THE UPGRADE
NINJA DUAL ZONE AIR FRYER
Cookbook UK

1800 Days Easy and Mouthwatering Ninja Foodi Recipes for Beginners with Tips & Tricks to Fry, Grill, and Bake

Sharron P. Jackson

All rights reserved.

Welcome to the world of [Sharron P. Jackson]'s culinary creations! We're thrilled to share our love for food through this recipe book, but before you start your culinary adventure, please take a moment to familiarize yourself with our copyright statement and disclaimer, which outline the guidelines for using this book.

This recipe book and its contents are protected by copyright law. Every recipe, photograph, and word within these pages represents our dedication to the art of cooking. We kindly ask that you honor our creativity by refraining from reproducing, storing, or distributing any part of this book without our prior written consent.

Cooking is a wonderful journey, but it's important to be aware of potential hazards. While we've taken every care to provide accurate and safe recipes, individual results may vary. We assume no responsibility for any accidents, injuries, or allergies that may occur while using this book. Exercise caution, follow food safety guidelines, and consult professionals as needed.

By using this recipe book, you agree to abide by the terms outlined in this copyright statement and disclaimer.

Thank you for choosing [Sharron P. Jackson]'s [The Upgrade Ninja Dual Zone Air Fryer Cookbook UK]. Your support is deeply appreciated, and we hope these recipes enrich your culinary experiences

UNLEASH YOUR CULINARY CREATIVITY!

Does this book inspire you to cook?

Do family and friends rave about your recipes?

DIY Your secret recipes in our cookbook now.

Date: _____

MY SHOPPING LIST

RECIPES

DATE

RECIPES	Salads	Meats	Soups
SERVES	Grains	Seafood	Snack
PREP TIME	Breads	Vegetables	Breakfast
COOK TIME	Appetizers	Desserts	Lunch
FROM THE KITCHEN OF	Main Dishes	Beverages	Dinners

INGREDIENTS

DIRECTIONS

NOTES

SERVING ☆☆☆☆☆

DIFFICULTY ☆☆☆☆☆

OVERALL ☆☆☆☆☆

CONTENTS

INTRODUCTION..7

Breakfast Recipes..9

Snacks And Appetizers Recipes....................18

Beef, Pork, And Lamb Recipes......................27

Poultry Recipes..36

Fish And Seafood Recipes.............................45

Vegetables And Sides Recipes......................54

Desserts Recipes..63

APPENDIX A: Measurement Conversions 72

Appendix B : Recipes Index..........................74

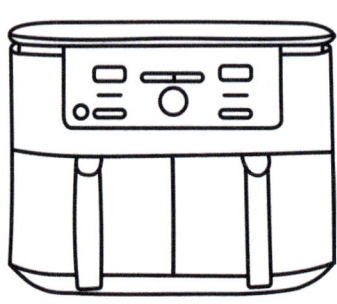

INTRODUCTION

I'm Sharron P. Jackson, and it is my absolute pleasure to welcome you to the Ninja Dual Zone Air Fryer Cookbook. As a seasoned culinary professional with over two decades of experience in the world of gastronomy, I've had the privilege of working in top-notch restaurants, hosting cooking shows, and honing my skills in kitchens around the globe. My culinary journey has been an incredible adventure, one filled with flavors, techniques, and a deep appreciation for the art of cooking.

So, why this cookbook? Well, it's rooted in my desire to bring the joy of cooking and the versatility of the Ninja Dual Zone Air Fryer to kitchens everywhere. Throughout my career, I've witnessed firsthand the transformative power of innovative kitchen appliances, and this air fryer is no exception. It's a marvel of modern cooking technology, capable of producing delicious, crispy results with a fraction of the oil traditionally used in frying.

The purpose of this cookbook is clear: to empower you, the home cook, to explore the full potential of the Ninja Dual Zone Air Fryer. Whether you're a seasoned chef or a kitchen novice, I'm here to guide you through a diverse array of recipes that span from classic comfort foods to international delights and even some creative, out-of-the-box dishes. These recipes are designed to be accessible, ensuring that you can whip up delectable meals for yourself, your family, and your friends.

This cookbook is a culmination of my passion for food, my professional experience, and my dedication to helping you elevate your culinary skills while embracing the convenience of the Ninja Dual Zone Air Fryer. I hope this collection of recipes becomes a source of inspiration and a gateway to your own culinary adventures. So, grab your apron, preheat your air fryer, and let's embark on this flavorful journey together!

WHAT ARE THE FEATURES OF NINJA DUAL ZONE AIR FRYER?

- Ninja Dual Zone Air Fryer offers two independent cooking zones for simultaneous cooking, saving time.

- Versatile cooking options include air frying, roasting, reheating, and dehydrating.

- User-friendly touchscreen controls and customizable cooking presets.

- High-capacity basket and rack for cooking larger meals.

- Rapid air circulation for crispy, golden results with less oil.

CLEANING TIPS FOR AIR FRYER

1. Wait for it to cool down completely.

2. Remove and clean the basket, tray, and any removable parts.

3. Wipe the interior with a damp cloth.

4. Clean the exterior with a damp cloth.

5. Regularly check and clean the heating element.

6. Use a non-abrasive sponge or brush.

7. Avoid using abrasive cleaners to prevent damage.

8. Refer to the manufacturer's cleaning instructions.

9. Clean the air vent to prevent blockage.

10. Keep it dry when not in use to prevent odors or rust.

YOUR AIR FRYER IS FOR MORE THAN FRYING

1. Baking: You can use an air fryer for baking tasks such as making muffins, cookies, or even small cakes. It's a convenient option for quick, single-serve baked goods.

2. Grilling: Many air fryers come with a grill pan or grill basket, allowing you to grill vegetables, seafood, or meat indoors without the need for an outdoor grill.

3. Roasting: Air fryers are excellent for roasting vegetables, meats, or poultry. The hot air circulates around the food, creating a crispy outer layer while keeping the inside tender and juicy.

4. Reheating: Reheating leftovers in an air fryer can restore their crispy texture, making them taste almost as good as freshly cooked.

5. Defrosting: Air fryers often have a defrosting function, which can safely and rapidly thaw frozen foods.

The air fryer's compact size, speed, and ability to cook with less oil make it a versatile and convenient addition to the kitchen, suitable for a wide range of cooking tasks beyond just frying.

Breakfast Recipes

Breakfast Bacon 10

Hash Browns 10

Banana And Raisins Muffins 11

Donuts 11

Crispy Hash Browns 12

Sausage With Eggs 12

Perfect Cinnamon Toast 13

Breakfast Frittata 13

Cinnamon-raisin Bagels Everything Bagels 14

Sweet Potato Hash 14

Healthy Oatmeal Muffins 15

Morning Egg Rolls 15

Spinach Egg Muffins 16

Egg White Muffins 16

Sweet Potatoes Hash 17

Baked Mushroom And Mozzarella Frittata With Breakfast Potatoes 17

Breakfast Recipes

Breakfast Bacon

Servings: 4 | Cooking Time: 14 Minutes.

Ingredients:
- ½ lb. bacon slices

Directions:
1. Spread half of the bacon slices in each of the crisper plate evenly in a single layer.
2. Return the crisper plate to the Ninja Foodi Dual Zone Air Fryer.
3. Choose the Air Fry mode for Zone 1 and set the temperature to 390 degrees F and the time to 14 minutes.
4. Select the "MATCH" button to copy the settings for Zone 2.
5. Initiate cooking by pressing the START/STOP button.
6. Flip the crispy bacon once cooked halfway through, then resume cooking.
7. Serve.

Nutrition Info:
- (Per serving) Calories 273 | Fat 22g | Sodium 517mg | Carbs 3.3g | Fiber 0.2g | Sugar 1.4g | Protein 16.1g

Hash Browns

Servings: 4 | Cooking Time: 5 Minutes

Ingredients:
- 4 frozen hash browns patties
- Cooking oil spray of choice

Directions:
1. Install a crisper plate in both drawers. Place half the hash browns in zone 1 and half in zone 2, then insert the drawers into the unit. Spray the hash browns with some cooking oil.
2. Select zone 1, select AIR FRY, set temperature to 390 degrees F/ 200 degrees C, and set time to 5 minutes.
3. Select MATCH to match zone 2 settings to zone 1. Press the START/STOP button to begin cooking.
4. When cooking is complete, remove the hash browns and serve.

Nutrition Info:
- (Per serving) Calories 130 | Fat 7g | Sodium 300mg | Carbs 15g | Fiber 2g | Sugar 0g | Protein 1g

Banana And Raisins Muffins

Servings:2 | Cooking Time:16

Ingredients:
- Salt, pinch
- 2 eggs, whisked
- 1/3 cup butter, melted
- 4 tablespoons of almond milk
- ¼ teaspoon of vanilla extract
- ½ teaspoon of baking powder
- 1-1/2 cup all-purpose flour
- 1 cup mashed bananas
- 2 tablespoons of raisins

Directions:
1. Take about 4 large (one-cup sized) ramekins and layer them with muffin papers.
2. Crack eggs in a large bowl, and whisk it all well and start adding vanilla extract, almond milk, baking powder, and melted butter
3. Whisk the ingredients very well.
4. Take a separate bowl and add the all-purpose flour, and salt.
5. Now, combine the add dry ingredients with the wet ingredients.
6. Now, pour mashed bananas and raisins into this batter
7. Mix it well to make a batter for the muffins.
8. Now pour the batter into four ramekins and divided the ramekins in the air fryer zones.
9. Set the timer for zone 1 to 16 minutes at 350 degrees F.
10. Select the MATCH button for the zone 2 basket.
11. Check if not done, and let it AIR FRY for one more minute.
12. Oncc it is done, serve.

Nutrition Info:
- (Per serving) Calories 727| Fat 43.1g| Sodium366 mg | Carbs 74.4g | Fiber 4.7g | Sugar 16.1g | Protein 14.1g

Donuts

Servings: 6 | Cooking Time: 15 Minutes

Ingredients:
- 1 cup granulated sugar
- 2 tablespoons ground cinnamon
- 1 can refrigerated flaky buttermilk biscuits
- ¼ cup unsalted butter, melted

Directions:
1. Combine the sugar and cinnamon in a small shallow bowl and set aside.
2. Remove the biscuits from the can and put them on a chopping board, separated. Cut holes in the center of each biscuit with a 1-inch round biscuit cutter (or a similarly sized bottle cap).
3. Place a crisper plate in each drawer. In each drawer, place 4 biscuits in a single layer. Insert the drawers into the unit.
4. Select zone 1, then AIR FRY, then set the temperature to 360 degrees F/ 180 degrees C with a 10-minute timer. To match zone 2 settings to zone 1, choose MATCH. To begin cooking, select START/STOP.
5. Remove the donuts from the drawers after the timer has finished.

Nutrition Info:
- (Per serving) Calories 223 | Fat 8g | Sodium 150mg | Carbs 40g | Fiber 1.4g | Sugar 34.2g | Protein 0.8g

Crispy Hash Browns

Servings: 4 | Cooking Time: 13 Minutes.

Ingredients:
- 3 russet potatoes
- ¼ cup chopped green peppers
- ¼ cup chopped red peppers
- ¼ cup chopped onions
- 2 garlic cloves chopped
- 1 teaspoon paprika
- Salt and black pepper, to taste
- 2 teaspoons olive oil

Directions:
1. Peel and grate all the potatoes with the help of a cheese grater.
2. Add potato shreds to a bowl filled with cold water and leave it soaked for 25 minutes.
3. Drain the water and place the potato shreds on a plate lined with a paper towel.
4. Transfer the shreds to a dry bowl and add olive oil, paprika, garlic, and black pepper.
5. Make four flat patties out of the potato mixture and place two into each of the crisper plate.
6. Return the crisper plate to the Ninja Foodi Dual Zone Air Fryer.
7. Choose the Air Fry mode for Zone 1 and set the temperature to 390 degrees F and set the time to 13 minutes.
8. Select the "MATCH" button to copy the settings for Zone 2.
9. Initiate cooking by pressing the START/STOP button.
10. Flip the potato hash browns once cooked halfway through, then resume cooking.
11. Once done, serve warm.

Nutrition Info:
- (Per serving) Calories 190 | Fat 18g | Sodium 150mg | Carbs 0.6g | Fiber 0.4g | Sugar 0.4g | Protein 7.2g

Sausage With Eggs

Servings: 2 | Cooking Time: 13

Ingredients:
- 4 sausage links, raw and uncooked
- 4 eggs, uncooked
- 1 tablespoon of green onion
- 2 tablespoons of chopped tomatoes
- Salt and black pepper, to taste
- 2 tablespoons of milk, dairy
- Oil spray, for greasing

Directions:
1. Take a bowl and whisk eggs in it.
2. Then pour milk, and add onions and tomatoes.
3. Whisk it all well.
4. Now season it with salt and black pepper.
5. Take one cake pan, that fit inside the air fryer and grease it with oil spray.
6. Pour the omelet in the greased cake pans.
7. Put the cake pan inside zone 1 air fryer basket of Ninja Foodie 2-Basket Air Fryer.
8. Now place the sausage link into the zone 2 basket.
9. Select bake for zone 1 basket and set the timer to 8-10 minutes at 300 degrees F.
10. For the zone 2 basket, select the AIR FRY button and set the timer to 12 minutes at 390 degrees.
11. Once the cooking cycle completes, serve by transferring it to plates.
12. Chop the sausage or cut it in round and then mix it with omelet.
13. Enjoy hot as a delicious breakfast.

Nutrition Info:
- (Per serving) Calories 240 | Fat 18.4g | Sodium 396mg | Carbs 2.8g | Fiber 0.2g | Sugar 2g | Protein 15.6g

Perfect Cinnamon Toast

Servings: 6 | Cooking Time: 10 Minutes

Ingredients:
- 12 slices whole-wheat bread
- 1 stick butter, room temperature
- ½ cup white sugar
- 1½ teaspoons ground cinnamon
- 1½ teaspoons pure vanilla extract
- 1 pinch kosher salt
- 2 pinches freshly ground black pepper (optional)

Directions:
1. Mash the softened butter with a fork or the back of a spoon in a bowl. Add the sugar, cinnamon, vanilla, and salt. Stir until everything is well combined.
2. Spread one-sixth of the mixture onto each slice of bread, making sure to cover the entire surface.
3. Install a crisper plate in both drawers. Place half the bread sliced in the zone 1 drawer and half in the zone 2 drawer, then insert the drawers into the unit.
4. Select zone 1, select AIR FRY, set temperature to 400 degrees F/ 200 degrees C, and set time to 5 minutes. Select MATCH to match zone 2 settings to zone 1. Press theSTART/STOP button to begin cooking
5. When cooking is complete, remove the slices and cut them diagonally.
6. Serve immediately.

Nutrition Info:
- (Per serving) Calories 322 | Fat 16.5g | Sodium 249mg | Carbs 39.3g | Fiber 4.2g | Sugar 18.2g | Protein 8.2g

Breakfast Frittata

Servings: 4 | Cooking Time: 12 Minutes

Ingredients:
- 4 eggs
- 4 tablespoons milk
- 35g cheddar cheese grated
- 50g feta crumbled
- 1 tomato, deseeded and chopped
- 15g spinach chopped
- 1 tablespoon fresh herbs, chopped
- 2 spring onion chopped
- Salt and black pepper, to taste
- ½ teaspoon olive oil

Directions:
1. Beat eggs with milk in a bowl and stir in the rest of the ingredients.
2. Grease two small-sized springform pans and line them with parchment paper.
3. Divide the egg mixture into the pans and place one in each air fryer basket.
4. Return the air fryer basket 1 to Zone 1, and basket 2 to Zone 2 of the Ninja Foodi 2-Basket Air Fryer.
5. Choose the "Air Fry" mode for Zone 1 at 350 degrees F and 12 minutes of cooking time.
6. Select the "MATCH COOK" option to copy the settings for Zone 2.
7. Initiate cooking by pressing the START/PAUSE BUTTON.
8. Serve warm.

Nutrition Info:
- (Per serving) Calories 273 | Fat 22g |Sodium 517mg | Carbs 3.3g | Fiber 0.2g | Sugar 1.4g | Protein 16.1g

Cinnamon-raisin Bagels Everything Bagels

Servings: 4 | Cooking Time: 14 Minutes

Ingredients:
- FOR THE BAGEL DOUGH
- 1 cup all-purpose flour, plus more for dusting
- 2 teaspoons baking powder
- 1 teaspoon kosher salt
- 1 cup reduced-fat plain Greek yogurt
- FOR THE CINNAMON-RAISIN BAGELS
- ¼ cup raisins
- ½ teaspoon ground cinnamon
- FOR THE EVERYTHING BAGELS
- ¼ teaspoon poppy seeds
- ¼ teaspoon sesame seeds
- ¼ teaspoon dried minced garlic
- ¼ teaspoon dried minced onion
- FOR THE EGG WASH
- 1 large egg
- 1 tablespoon water

Directions:
1. To prep the bagels: In a large bowl, combine the flour, baking powder, and salt. Stir in the yogurt to form a soft dough. Turn the dough out onto a lightly floured surface and knead five to six times, until it is smooth and elastic. Divide the dough in half.
2. Knead the raisins and cinnamon into one dough half. Leave the other dough half plain.
3. Divide both portions of dough in half to form a total of 4 balls of dough (2 cinnamon-raisin and 2 plain). Roll each ball of dough into a rope about 8 inches long. Shape each rope into a ring and pinch the ends to seal.
4. To prep the everything bagels: In a small bowl, mix together the poppy seeds, sesame seeds, garlic, and onion.
5. To prep the egg wash: In a second small bowl, beat together the egg and water. Brush the egg wash on top of each bagel.
6. Generously sprinkle the everything seasoning over the top of the 2 plain bagels.
7. To cook the bagels: Install a crisper plate in each of the two baskets. Place the cinnamon-raisin bagels in the Zone 1 basket and insert the basket in the unit. For best results, the bagels should not overlap in the basket. Place the everything bagels in the Zone 2 basket and insert the basket in the unit.
8. Select Zone 1, select AIR FRY, set the temperature to 325°F, and set the time to 14 minutes. Select MATCH COOK to match Zone 2 settings to Zone 1.
9. Press START/PAUSE to begin cooking.
10. When cooking is complete, use silicone-tipped tongs to transfer the bagels to a cutting board. Let cool for 2 to 3 minutes before cutting and serving.

Nutrition Info:
- (Per serving) Calories: 238; Total fat: 3g; Saturated fat: 1g; Carbohydrates: 43g; Fiber: 1.5g; Protein: 11g; Sodium: 321mg

Sweet Potato Hash

Servings: 4 | Cooking Time: 15 Minutes

Ingredients:
- 3 sweet potatoes, peel & cut into ½-inch pieces
- ½ tsp cinnamon
- 2 tbsp olive oil
- 1 bell pepper, cut into ½-inch pieces
- ½ tsp dried thyme
- ½ tsp nutmeg
- 1 medium onion, cut into ½-inch pieces
- Pepper
- Salt

Directions:
1. In a bowl, toss sweet potatoes with the remaining ingredients.
2. Insert a crisper plate in Ninja Foodi air fryer baskets.
3. Add potato mixture in both baskets.
4. Select zone 1 then select "air fry" mode and set the temperature to 355 degrees F for 15 minutes. Press "match" to match zone 2 settings to zone 1. Press "start/stop" to begin.

Nutrition Info:
- (Per serving) Calories 167 | Fat 7.3g | Sodium 94mg | Carbs 24.9g | Fiber 4.2g | Sugar 6.8g | Protein 2.2g

Healthy Oatmeal Muffins

Servings: 6 | Cooking Time: 17 Minutes

Ingredients:
- 1 egg
- ¼ tsp ground ginger
- 1 tsp ground cinnamon
- ½ tsp baking soda
- ½ tsp baking powder
- 55g brown sugar
- ½ tsp vanilla
- 2 tbsp butter, melted
- 125g applesauce
- 61ml milk
- 68gm whole wheat flour
- 100gm quick oats
- Pinch of salt

Directions:
1. In a mixing bowl, mix together all dry the ingredients.
2. In a separate bowl, add the remaining ingredients and mix well.
3. Add the dry ingredients mixture into the wet mixture and mix until well combined.
4. Pour the batter into the silicone muffin moulds.
5. Insert a crisper plate in the Ninja Foodi air fryer baskets.
6. Place muffin moulds in both baskets.
7. Select zone 1 then select "bake" mode and set the temperature to 390 degrees F for 17 minutes. Press "start/stop" to begin.

Nutrition Info:
- (Per serving) Calories 173 | Fat 5.8g | Sodium 177mg | Carbs 26.6g | Fiber 2.1g | Sugar 8.7g | Protein 4.2g

Morning Egg Rolls

Servings: 6 | Cooking Time: 13 Minutes.

Ingredients:
- 2 eggs
- 2 tablespoons milk
- Salt, to taste
- Black pepper, to taste
- ½ cup shredded cheddar cheese
- 2 sausage patties
- 6 egg roll wrappers
- 1 tablespoon olive oil
- 1 cup water

Directions:
1. Grease a small skillet with some olive oil and place it over medium heat.
2. Add sausage patties and cook them until brown.
3. Chop the cooked patties into small pieces. Beat eggs with salt, black pepper, and milk in a mixing bowl.
4. Grease the same skillet with 1 teaspoon of olive oil and pour the egg mixture into it.
5. Stir cook to make scrambled eggs.
6. Add sausage, mix well and remove the skillet from the heat.
7. Spread an egg roll wrapper on the working surface in a diamond shape position.
8. Add a tablespoon of cheese at the bottom third of the roll wrapper.
9. Top the cheese with egg mixture and wet the edges of the wrapper with water.
10. Fold the two corners of the wrapper and roll it, then seal the edges.
11. Repeat the same steps and divide the rolls in the two crisper plates.
12. Return the crisper plates to the Ninja Foodi Dual Zone Air Fryer.
13. Choose the Air Fry mode for Zone 1 and set the temperature to 375 degrees F and the time to 13 minutes.
14. Select the "MATCH" button to copy the settings for Zone 2.
15. Initiate cooking by pressing the START/STOP button.
16. Flip the rolls after 8 minutes and continue cooking for another 5 minutes.
17. Serve warm and fresh.

Nutrition Info:
- (Per serving) Calories 282 | Fat 15g | Sodium 526mg | Carbs 20g | Fiber 0.6g | Sugar 3.3g | Protein 16g

Spinach Egg Muffins

Servings: 4 | Cooking Time: 13 Minutes.

Ingredients:
- 4 tablespoons milk
- 4 tablespoons frozen spinach, thawed
- 4 large eggs
- 8 teaspoons grated cheese
- Salt, to taste
- Black pepper, to taste
- Cooking Spray

Directions:
1. Grease four small-sized ramekin with cooking spray.
2. Add egg, cheese, spinach, and milk to a bowl and beat well.
3. Divide the mixture into the four small ramekins and top them with salt and black pepper.
4. Place the two ramekins in each of the two crisper plate.
5. Return the crisper plate to the Ninja Foodi Dual Zone Air Fryer.
6. Choose the Air Fry mode for Zone 1 and set the temperature to 390 degrees F and the time to 13 minutes.
7. Select the "MATCH" button to copy the settings for Zone 2.
8. Initiate cooking by pressing the START/STOP button.
9. Serve warm.

Nutrition Info:
- (Per serving) Calories 237 | Fat 19g | Sodium 518mg | Carbs 7g | Fiber 1.5g | Sugar 3.4g | Protein 12g

Egg White Muffins

Servings: 8 | Cooking Time: 10 Minutes

Ingredients:
- 4 slices center-cut bacon, cut into strips
- 4 ounces baby bella mushrooms, roughly chopped
- 2 ounces sun-dried tomatoes
- 2 tablespoon sliced black olives
- 2 tablespoons grated or shredded parmesan
- 2 tablespoons shredded mozzarella
- ¼ teaspoon black pepper
- ¾ cup liquid egg whites
- 2 tablespoons liquid egg whites

Directions:
1. Heat a saucepan with a little oil, add the bacon and mushrooms and cook until fully cooked and crispy, about 6–8 minutes.
2. While the bacon and mushrooms cook, mix the ¾ cup liquid egg whites, sun-dried tomato, olives, parmesan, mozzarella, and black pepper together in a large bowl.
3. Add the cooked bacon and mushrooms to the tomato and olive mixture, stirring everything together.
4. Spoon the mixture into muffin molds, followed by 2 tablespoons of egg whites over the top.
5. Place half the muffins mold in zone 1 and half in zone 2, then insert the drawers into the unit.
6. Select zone 1, select AIR FRY, set temperature to 390 degrees F/ 200 degrees C, and set time to 22 minutes.
7. Select MATCH to match zone 2 settings to zone 1. Press the START/STOP button to begin cooking.
8. When cooking is complete, remove the molds and enjoy!

Nutrition Info:
- (Per serving) Calories 104 | Fat 5.6g | Sodium 269mg | Carbs 3.5g | Fiber 0.8g | Sugar 0.3g | Protein 10.3g

Sweet Potatoes Hash

Servings:2 | Cooking Time:25

Ingredients:
- 450 grams sweet potatoes
- 1/2 white onion, diced
- 3 tablespoons of olive oil
- 1 teaspoon smoked paprika
- 1/4 teaspoon cumin
- 1/3 teaspoon of ground turmeric
- 1/4 teaspoon of garlic salt
- 1 cup guacamole

Directions:
1. Peel and cut the potatoes into cubes.
2. Now, transfer the potatoes to a bowl and add oil, white onions, cumin, paprika, turmeric, and garlic salt.
3. Put this mixture between both the baskets of the Ninja Foodie 2-Basket Air Fryer.
4. Set it to AIR FRY mode for 10 minutes at 390 degrees F.
5. Then take out the baskets and shake them well.
6. Then again set time to 15 minutes at 390 degrees F.
7. Once done, serve it with guacamole.

Nutrition Info:
- (Per serving) Calories691 | Fat 49.7g| Sodium 596mg | Carbs 64g | Fiber15g | Sugar 19g | Protein 8.1g

Baked Mushroom And Mozzarella Frittata With Breakfast Potatoes

Servings:4 | Cooking Time: 35 Minutes

Ingredients:
- FOR THE FRITTATA
- 8 large eggs
- ⅓ cup whole milk
- 1 teaspoon kosher salt
- ½ teaspoon freshly ground black pepper
- 1 cup sliced cremini mushrooms (about 2 ounces)
- 1 teaspoon olive oil
- 2 ounces part-skim mozzarella cheese, cut into ½-inch cubes
- FOR THE POTATOES
- 2 russet potatoes, cut into ½-inch cubes
- 1 tablespoon olive oil
- ½ teaspoon garlic powder
- ¼ teaspoon kosher salt
- ¼ teaspoon freshly ground black pepper

Directions:
1. To prep the frittata: In a large bowl, whisk together the eggs, milk, salt, and pepper. Stir in the mushrooms.
2. To prep the potatoes: In a large bowl, combine the potatoes, olive oil, garlic powder, salt, and black pepper.
3. To cook the frittata and potatoes: Brush the bottom of the Zone 1 basket with 1 teaspoon of olive oil. Add the egg mixture to the basket, top with the mozzarella cubes, and insert the basket in the unit. Install a crisper plate in the Zone 2 basket. Place the potatoes in the basket and insert the basket in the unit.
4. Select Zone 1, select BAKE, set the temperature to 350°F, and set the time to 30 minutes.
5. Select Zone 2, select AIR FRY, set the temperature to 400°F, and set the time to 35 minutes. Select SMART FINISH.
6. Press START/PAUSE to begin cooking.
7. When the Zone 2 timer reads 15 minutes, press START/PAUSE. Remove the basket and shake the potatoes for 10 seconds. Reinsert the basket and press START/PAUSE to resume cooking.
8. When cooking is complete, the frittata will pull away from the edges of the basket and the potatoes will be golden brown. Transfer the frittata to a cutting board and cut into 4 portions. Serve with the potatoes.

Nutrition Info:
- (Per serving) Calories: 307; Total fat: 17g; Saturated fat: 5.5g; Carbohydrates: 18g; Fiber: 1g; Protein: 19g; Sodium: 600mg

Snacks And Appetizers Recipes

Peppered Asparagus 19

Cauliflower Cheese Patties 19

Cauliflower Gnocchi 20

Onion Rings 20

Bacon-wrapped Dates Bacon-wrapped Scallops 21

Potato Tater Tots 21

Avocado Fries With Sriracha Dip 22

Cinnamon Sugar Chickpeas 22

Stuffed Mushrooms 23

Tofu Veggie Meatballs 23

Fried Ravioli 24

Crab Rangoon Dip With Crispy Wonton Strips 24

Sweet Bites 25

Beef Jerky Pineapple Jerky 25

Cheese Stuffed Mushrooms 26

Crispy Popcorn Shrimp 26

Snacks And Appetizers Recipes

Peppered Asparagus

Servings: 6 | Cooking Time: 16 Minutes.

Ingredients:
- 1 bunch of asparagus, trimmed
- Avocado or Olive Oil
- Himalayan salt, to taste
- Black pepper, to taste

Directions:
1. Divide the asparagus in the two crisper plate.
2. Toss the asparagus with salt, black pepper, and oil.
3. Return the crisper plate to the Ninja Foodi Dual Zone Air Fryer.
4. Choose the Air Fry mode for Zone 1 and set the temperature to 390 degrees F and the time to 16 minutes.
5. Select the "MATCH" button to copy the settings for Zone 2.
6. Initiate cooking by pressing the START/STOP button.
7. Serve warm.

Nutrition Info:
- (Per serving) Calories 163 | Fat 11.5g | Sodium 918mg | Carbs 8.3g | Fiber 4.2g | Sugar 0.2g | Protein 7.4g

Cauliflower Cheese Patties

Servings: 4 | Cooking Time: 10 Minutes

Ingredients:
- 2 eggs
- 200g cauliflower rice, microwave for 5 minutes
- 56g mozzarella cheese, shredded
- 22g parmesan cheese, grated
- 11g Mexican cheese, shredded
- ½ tsp onion powder
- 1 tsp dried basil
- 1 tsp garlic powder
- 33g breadcrumbs
- Pepper
- Salt

Directions:
1. Add cauliflower rice and remaining ingredients into the mixing bowl and mix until well combined.
2. Insert a crisper plate in the Ninja Foodi air fryer baskets.
3. Make patties from the cauliflower mixture and place them in both baskets.
4. Select zone 1, then select "air fry" mode and set the temperature to 390 degrees F for 10 minutes. Press "match" to match zone 2 settings to zone 1. Press "start/stop" to begin. Turn halfway through.

Nutrition Info:
- (Per serving) Calories 318 | Fat 18g | Sodium 951mg | Carbs 11.1g | Fiber 1.8g | Sugar 2.2g | Protein 25.6g

Cauliflower Gnocchi

Servings: 5 | Cooking Time: 17 Minutes.

Ingredients:
- 1 bag frozen cauliflower gnocchi
- 1 ½ tablespoons olive oil
- 1 teaspoon garlic powder
- 3 tablespoons parmesan, grated
- ½ teaspoon dried basil
- Salt to taste
- Fresh chopped parsley for topping

Directions:
1. Toss gnocchi with olive oil, garlic powder, 1 tablespoon of parmesan, salt, and basil in a bowl.
2. Divide the gnocchi in the two crisper plate.
3. Return the crisper plate to the Ninja Foodi Dual Zone Air Fryer.
4. Choose the Air Fry mode for Zone 1 and set the temperature to 400 degrees F and the time to 10 minutes.
5. Select the "MATCH" button to copy the settings for Zone 2.
6. Initiate cooking by pressing the START/STOP button.
7. Toss the gnocchi once cooked halfway through, then resume cooking.
8. Drizzle the remaining parmesan on top of the gnocchi and cook again for 7 minutes.
9. Serve warm.

Nutrition Info:
- (Per serving) Calories 134 | Fat 5.9g | Sodium 343mg | Carbs 9.5g | Fiber 0.5g | Sugar 1.1g | Protein 10.4g

Onion Rings

Servings: 4 | Cooking Time: 7 Minutes

Ingredients:
- 170g onion, sliced into rings
- ½ cup breadcrumbs
- 2 eggs, beaten
- ½ cup flour
- Salt and black pepper to taste

Directions:
1. Mix flour, black pepper and salt in a bowl.
2. Dredge the onion rings through the flour mixture.
3. Dip them in the eggs and coat with the breadcrumbs.
4. Place the coated onion rings in the air fryer baskets.
5. Return the air fryer basket 1 to Zone 1, and basket 2 to Zone 2 of the Ninja Foodi 2-Basket Air Fryer.
6. Choose the "Air Fry" mode for Zone 1 at 350 degrees F and 7 minutes of cooking time.
7. Select the "MATCH COOK" option to copy the settings for Zone 2.
8. Initiate cooking by pressing the START/PAUSE BUTTON.
9. Shake the rings once cooked halfway through.
10. Serve warm.

Nutrition Info:
- (Per serving) Calories 185 | Fat 11g | Sodium 355mg | Carbs 21g | Fiber 5.8g | Sugar 3g | Protein 4.7g

Bacon-wrapped Dates Bacon-wrapped Scallops

Servings: 6 | Cooking Time: 12 Minutes

Ingredients:
- FOR THE SCALLOPS
- 6 slices bacon, halved crosswise
- 12 large sea scallops, patted dry
- FOR THE DATES
- 4 slices bacon, cut into thirds
- 12 pitted dates

Directions:
1. To prep the dates: Wrap each piece of bacon around a date and secure with a toothpick.
2. To cook the dates and the bacon for the scallops: Install a crisper plate in each of the two baskets. Place the bacon for the scallops in the Zone 1 basket in a single layer and insert the basket in the unit. Place the bacon-wrapped dates in the Zone 2 basket in a single layer and insert the basket in the unit.
3. Select Zone 1, select AIR FRY, set the temperature to 400°F, and set the time to 12 minutes.
4. Select Zone 2, select AIR FRY, set the temperature to 360°F, and set the time to 10 minutes. Select SMART FINISH.
5. Press START/PAUSE to begin cooking.
6. When the Zone 1 timer reads 9 minutes, press START/PAUSE. Remove the basket from the unit. Wrap each piece of bacon around a scallop and secure with a toothpick. Place the bacon-wrapped scallops in the basket. Reinsert the basket and press START/PAUSE to resume cooking.
7. When the Zone 1 timer reads 4 minutes, press START/PAUSE. Remove the basket and use silicone-tipped tongs to flip the scallops. Reinsert the basket and press START/PAUSE to resume cooking.
8. When cooking is complete, the scallops will be opaque and the bacon around both the scallops and dates will be crisp. Arrange the bacon-wrapped scallops and dates on a serving platter. Serve warm.

Nutrition Info:
- (Per serving) Calories: 191; Total fat: 2.5g; Saturated fat: 1g; Carbohydrates: 39g; Fiber: 4g; Protein: 3g; Sodium: 115mg

Potato Tater Tots

Servings: 4 | Cooking Time: 27 Minutes.

Ingredients:
- 2 potatoes, peeled
- ½ teaspoon Cajun seasoning
- Olive oil cooking spray
- Sea salt to taste

Directions:
1. Boil water in a cooking pot and cook potatoes in it for 15 minutes.
2. Drain and leave the potatoes to cool in a bowl.
3. Grate these potatoes and toss them with Cajun seasoning.
4. Make small tater tots out of this mixture.
5. Divide them into the two crisper plates and spray them with cooking oil.
6. Return the crisper plates to the Ninja Foodi Dual Zone Air Fryer.
7. Choose the Air Fry mode for Zone 1 and set the temperature to 375 degrees F and the time to 27 minutes.
8. Select the "MATCH" button to copy the settings for Zone 2.
9. Initiate cooking by pressing the START/STOP button.
10. Flip them once cooked halfway through, and resume cooking.
11. Serve warm

Nutrition Info:
- (Per serving) Calories 185 | Fat 11g | Sodium 355mg | Carbs 21g | Fiber 5.8g | Sugar 3g | Protein 4.7g

Avocado Fries With Sriracha Dip

Servings: 4 | Cooking Time: 6 Minutes

Ingredients:
- Avocado Fries
- 4 avocados, peeled and cut into sticks
- ¾ cup panko breadcrumbs
- ¼ cup flour
- 2 eggs, beaten
- ½ teaspoon garlic powder
- ½ teaspoon salt
- SRIRACHA-RANCH SAUCE
- ¼ cup ranch dressing
- 1 teaspoon sriracha sauce

Directions:
1. Mix flour with garlic powder and salt in a bowl.
2. Dredge the avocado sticks through the flour mixture.
3. Dip them in the eggs and coat them with breadcrumbs.
4. Place the coated fries in the air fryer baskets.
5. Return the air fryer basket 1 to Zone 1, and basket 2 to Zone 2 of the Ninja Foodi 2-Basket Air Fryer.
6. Choose the "Air Fry" mode for Zone 1 at 400 degrees F and 6 minutes of cooking time.
7. Select the "MATCH COOK" option to copy the settings for Zone 2.
8. Initiate cooking by pressing the START/PAUSE BUTTON.
9. Flip the fries once cooked halfway through.
10. Mix all the dipping sauce ingredients in a bowl.
11. Serve the fries with dipping sauce.

Nutrition Info:
- (Per serving) Calories 229 | Fat 1.9 | Sodium 567mg | Carbs 1.9g | Fiber 0.4g | Sugar 0.6g | Protein 11.8g

Cinnamon Sugar Chickpeas

Servings: 4 | Cooking Time: 15 Minutes

Ingredients:
- 2 cups chickpeas, drained
- Spray oil
- 1 tablespoon coconut sugar
- ½ teaspoon cinnamon
- Serving
- 57g cheddar cheese, cubed
- ¼ cup raw almonds
- 85g jerky, sliced

Directions:
1. Toss chickpeas with coconut sugar, cinnamon and oil in a bowl.
2. Divide the chickpeas into the Ninja Foodi 2 Baskets Air Fryer baskets.
3. Drizzle cheddar cheese, almonds and jerky on top.
4. Return the air fryer basket 1 to Zone 1, and basket 2 to Zone 2 of the Ninja Foodi 2-Basket Air Fryer.
5. Choose the "Air Fry" mode for Zone 1 at 380 degrees F and 15 minutes of cooking time.
6. Select the "MATCH COOK" option to copy the settings for Zone 2.
7. Initiate cooking by pressing the START/PAUSE BUTTON.
8. Toss the chickpeas once cooked halfway through.
9. Serve warm.

Nutrition Info:
- (Per serving) Calories 103 | Fat 8.4g | Sodium 117mg | Carbs 3.5g | Fiber 0.9g | Sugar 1.5g | Protein 5.1g

Stuffed Mushrooms

Servings: 5 | Cooking Time: 8 Minutes

Ingredients:
- 8 ounces fresh mushrooms (I used Monterey)
- 4 ounces cream cheese
- ¼ cup shredded parmesan cheese
- ⅛ cup shredded sharp cheddar cheese
- ⅛ cup shredded white cheddar cheese
- 1 teaspoon Worcestershire sauce
- 2 garlic cloves, minced
- Salt and pepper, to taste

Directions:
1. To prepare the mushrooms for stuffing, remove their stems. Make a circle cut around the area where the stem used to be. Continue to cut until all of the superfluous mushroom is removed.
2. To soften the cream cheese, microwave it for 15 seconds.
3. Combine the cream cheese, shredded cheeses, salt, pepper, garlic, and Worcestershire sauce in a medium mixing bowl. To blend, stir everything together.
4. Stuff the mushrooms with the cheese mixture.
5. Place a crisper plate in each drawer. Put the stuffed mushrooms in a single layer in each drawer. Insert the drawers into the unit.
6. Select zone 1, then AIR FRY, then set the temperature to 360 degrees F/ 180 degrees C with an 8-minute timer. To match zone 2 settings to zone 1, choose MATCH. To begin, select START/STOP.
7. Serve and enjoy!

Nutrition Info:
- (Per serving) Calories 230 | Fat 9.5g | Sodium 105mg | Carbs 35.5g | Fiber 5.1g | Sugar 0.1g | Protein 7.1g

Tofu Veggie Meatballs

Servings: 4 | Cooking Time: 10 minutes

Ingredients:
- 122g firm tofu, drained
- 50g breadcrumbs
- 37g bamboo shoots, thinly sliced
- 22g carrots, shredded & steamed
- 1 tsp garlic powder
- 1 ½ tbsp soy sauce
- 2 tbsp cornstarch
- 3 dried shitake mushrooms, soaked & chopped
- Pepper
- Salt

Directions:
1. Add tofu and remaining ingredients into the food processor and process until well combined.
2. Insert a crisper plate in the Ninja Foodi air fryer baskets.
3. Make small balls from the tofu mixture and place them in both baskets.
4. Select zone 1, then select "air fry" mode and set the temperature to 380 degrees F for 10 minutes. Press "match" to match zone 2 settings to zone 1. Press "start/stop" to begin. Turn halfway through.

Nutrition Info:
- (Per serving) Calories 125 | Fat 1.8g | Sodium 614mg | Carbs 23.4g | Fiber 2.5g | Sugar 3.8g | Protein 5.3g

Fried Ravioli

Servings: 6 | Cooking Time: 7 Minutes

Ingredients:
- 12 frozen raviolis
- 118ml buttermilk
- ½ cup Italian breadcrumbs

Directions:
1. Dip the ravioli in the buttermilk then coat with the breadcrumbs.
2. Divide the ravioli into the Ninja Foodi 2 Baskets Air Fryer baskets.
3. Return the air fryer basket 1 to Zone 1, and basket 2 to Zone 2 of the Ninja Foodi 2-Basket Air Fryer.
4. Choose the "Air Fry" mode for Zone 1 and set the temperature to 400 degrees F and 7 minutes of cooking time.
5. Select the "MATCH COOK" option to copy the settings for Zone 2.
6. Initiate cooking by pressing the START/PAUSE BUTTON.
7. Flip the ravioli once cooked halfway through.
8. Serve warm.

Nutrition Info:
- (Per serving) Calories 134 | Fat 5.9g | Sodium 343mg | Carbs 9.5g | Fiber 0.5g | Sugar 1.1g | Protein 10.4g

Crab Rangoon Dip With Crispy Wonton Strips

Servings: 6 | Cooking Time: 15 Minutes

Ingredients:
- FOR THE DIP
- 1 (6-ounce) can pink crab, drained
- 8 ounces (16 tablespoons) cream cheese, at room temperature
- ½ cup sour cream
- 1 tablespoon chopped scallions
- ½ teaspoon garlic powder
- 1 teaspoon Worcestershire sauce
- ¼ teaspoon kosher salt
- 1 cup shredded part-skim mozzarella cheese
- FOR THE WONTON STRIPS
- 12 wonton wrappers
- 1 tablespoon olive oil
- ¼ teaspoon kosher salt

Directions:
1. To prep the dip: In a medium bowl, mix the crab, cream cheese, sour cream, scallions, garlic powder, Worcestershire sauce, and salt until smooth.
2. To prep the wonton strips: Brush both sides of the wonton wrappers with the oil and sprinkle with salt. Cut the wonton wrappers into ¾-inch-wide strips.
3. To cook the dip and strips: Pour the dip into the Zone 1 basket, top with the mozzarella cheese, and insert the basket in the unit. Install a crisper plate in the Zone 2 basket, add the wonton strips, and insert the basket in the unit.
4. Select Zone 1, select BAKE, set the temperature to 330°F, and set the time to 15 minutes.
5. Select Zone 2, select AIR FRY, set the temperature to 350°F, and set the time to 6 minutes. Select SMART FINISH.
6. Press START/PAUSE to begin cooking.
7. When the Zone 2 timer reads 4 minutes, press START/PAUSE. Remove the basket and shake well to redistribute the wonton strips. Reinsert the basket and press START/PAUSE to resume cooking.
8. When the Zone 2 timer reads 2 minutes, press START/PAUSE. Remove the basket and shake well to redistribute the wonton strips. Reinsert the basket and press START/PAUSE to resume cooking.
9. When cooking is complete, the dip will be bubbling and golden brown on top and the wonton strips will be crunchy. Serve warm.

Nutrition Info:
- (Per serving) Calories: 315; Total fat: 23g; Saturated fat: 12g; Carbohydrates: 14g; Fiber: 0.5g; Protein: 14g; Sodium: 580mg

Sweet Bites

Servings:4 | Cooking Time:12

Ingredients:
- 10 sheets of Phyllo dough, (filo dough)
- 2 tablespoons of melted butter
- 1 cup walnuts, chopped
- 2 teaspoons of honey
- Pinch of cinnamon
- 1 teaspoon of orange zest

Directions:
1. First, layer together 10 Phyllo dough sheets on a flat surface.
2. Then cut it into 4 *4-inch squares.
3. Now, coat the squares with butter, drizzle some honey, orange zest, walnuts, and cinnamon.
4. Bring all 4 corners together and press the corners to make a little like purse design.
5. Divide it amongst air fryer basket and select zone 1 basket using AIR fry mode and set it for 7 minutes at 375 degrees F.
6. Select the MATCH button for the zone 2 basket.
7. Once done, take out and serve.

Nutrition Info:
- (Per serving) Calories 397| Fat 27.1 g| Sodium 271mg | Carbs31.2 g | Fiber 3.2g| Sugar3.3g | Protein 11g

Beef Jerky Pineapple Jerky

Servings:8 | Cooking Time: 6 To 12 Hours

Ingredients:
- FOR THE BEEF JERKY
- ½ cup reduced-sodium soy sauce
- ¼ cup pineapple juice
- 1 tablespoon dark brown sugar
- 1 tablespoon Worcestershire sauce
- ½ teaspoon smoked paprika
- ¼ teaspoon freshly ground black pepper
- ¼ teaspoon red pepper flakes
- 1 pound beef bottom round, trimmed of excess fat, cut into ¼-inch-thick slices
- FOR THE PINEAPPLE JERKY
- 1 pound pineapple, cut into ⅛-inch-thick rounds, pat dry
- 1 teaspoon chili powder (optional)

Directions:
1. To prep the beef jerky: In a large zip-top bag, combine the soy sauce, pineapple juice, brown sugar, Worcestershire sauce, smoked paprika, black pepper, and red pepper flakes.
2. Add the beef slices, seal the bag, and toss to coat the meat in the marinade. Refrigerate overnight or for at least 8 hours.
3. Remove the beef slices and discard the marinade. Using a paper towel, pat the slices dry to remove excess marinade.
4. To prep the pineapple jerky: Sprinkle the pineapple with chili powder (if using).
5. To dehydrate the jerky: Arrange half of the beef slices in a single layer in the Zone 1 basket, making sure they do not overlap. Place a crisper plate on top of the beef slices and arrange the remaining slices in a single layer on top of the crisper plate. Insert the basket in the unit.
6. Repeat this process with the pineapple in the Zone 2 basket and insert the basket in the unit.
7. Select Zone 1, select DEHYDRATE, set the temperature to 150°F, and set the time to 8 hours.
8. Select Zone 2, select DEHYDRATE, set the temperature to 135°F, and set the time to 12 hours.
9. Press START/PAUSE to begin cooking.
10. When the Zone 1 timer reads 2 hours, press START/PAUSE. Remove the basket and check the beef jerky for doneness. If necessary, reinsert the basket and press START/PAUSE to resume cooking.

Nutrition Info:
- (Per serving) Calories: 171; Total fat: 6.5g; Saturated fat: 2g; Carbohydrates: 2g; Fiber: 0g; Protein: 25g; Sodium: 369mg

Cheese Stuffed Mushrooms

Servings: 4 | Cooking Time: 8 Minutes

Ingredients:
- 176g button mushrooms, clean & cut stems
- 46g sour cream
- 17g cream cheese, softened
- ½ tsp garlic powder
- 58g cheddar cheese, shredded
- Pepper
- Salt

Directions:
1. In a small bowl, mix cream cheese, garlic powder, sour cream, pepper, and salt.
2. Stuff cream cheese mixture into each mushroom and top each with cheddar cheese.
3. Insert a crisper plate in the Ninja Foodi air fryer baskets.
4. Place the stuffed mushrooms in both baskets.
5. Select zone 1 then select "air fry" mode and set the temperature to 370 degrees F for 8 minutes. Press "match" to match zone 2 settings to zone 1. Press "start/stop" to begin.

Nutrition Info:
- (Per serving) Calories 222 | Fat 19.4g | Sodium 220mg | Carbs 5.6g | Fiber 1.2g | Sugar 2.2g | Protein 8.9g

Crispy Popcorn Shrimp

Servings: 4 | Cooking Time: 6 Minutes

Ingredients:
- 170g shrimp, peeled and diced
- ½ cup breadcrumbs
- Salt and black pepper to taste
- 2 eggs, beaten

Directions:
1. Mix breadcrumbs with black pepper and salt in a bowl.
2. Dip the shrimp pieces in the eggs and coat each with breadcrumbs.
3. Divide the shrimp popcorn into the 2 Air Fryer baskets.
4. Return the air fryer basket 1 to Zone 1, and basket 2 to Zone 2 of the Ninja Foodi 2-Basket Air Fryer.
5. Choose the "Air Fry" mode for Zone 1 at 400 degrees F and 6 minutes of cooking time.
6. Select the "MATCH COOK" option to copy the settings for Zone 2.
7. Initiate cooking by pressing the START/PAUSE BUTTON.
8. Serve warm.

Nutrition Info:
- (Per serving) Calories 180 | Fat 3.2g | Sodium 133mg | Carbs 32g | Fiber 1.1g | Sugar 1.8g | Protein 9g

Beef, Pork, And Lamb Recipes

- Spicy Lamb Chops 28
- Steak In Air Fry 28
- Beef & Broccoli 29
- Meatballs 29
- Curry-crusted Lamb Chops With Baked Brown Sugar Acorn Squash 30
- Italian Sausages With Peppers, Potatoes, And Onions 30
- Pork With Green Beans And Potatoes 31
- Glazed Steak Recipe 31
- Short Ribs & Root Vegetables 32
- Italian-style Meatballs With Garlicky Roasted Broccoli 32
- Mustard Rubbed Lamb Chops 33
- Beef Kofta Kebab 33
- Marinated Pork Chops 34
- Lamb Chops With Dijon Garlic 34
- Chinese Bbq Pork 35
- Marinated Steak & Mushrooms 35

Beef, Pork, And Lamb Recipes

Spicy Lamb Chops

Servings:4 | Cooking Time:15

Ingredients:
- 12 lamb chops, bone-in
- Salt and black pepper, to taste
- ½ teaspoon of lemon zest
- 1 tablespoon of lemon juice
- 1 teaspoon of paprika
- 1 teaspoon of garlic powder
- ½ teaspoon of Italian seasoning
- ¼ teaspoon of onion powder

Directions:
1. Add the lamb chops to the bowl and sprinkle salt, garlic powder, Italian seasoning, onion powder, black pepper, lemon zest, lemon juice, and paprika.
2. Rub the chops well, and divide it between both the baskets of the air fryer.
3. Set zone 1 basket to 400 degrees F, for 15 minutes at AIR FRY mode.
4. Select MATCH for zone2 basket.
5. After 10 minutes, take out the baskets and flip the chops cook for the remaining minutes, and then serve.

Nutrition Info:
- (Per serving) Calories 787| Fat 45.3g| Sodium1 mg | Carbs 16.1g | Fiber0.3g | Sugar 0.4g | Protein 75.3g

Steak In Air Fry

Servings:1 | Cooking Time:20

Ingredients:
- 2 teaspoons of canola oil
- 1 tablespoon of Montreal steaks seasoning
- 1 pound of beef steak

Directions:
1. The first step is to season the steak on both sides with canola oil and then rub a generous amount of steak seasoning all over.
2. We are using the AIR BROIL feature of the ninja air fryer and it works with one basket.
3. Put the steak in the basket and set it to AIR BROIL at 450 degrees F for 20 -22 minutes.
4. After 7 minutes, hit pause and take out the basket to flip the steak, and cover it with foil on top, for the remaining 14 minutes.
5. Once done, serve the medium-rare steak and enjoy it by resting for 10 minutes.
6. Serve by cutting in slices.
7. Enjoy.

Nutrition Info:
- (Per serving) Calories 935| Fat 37.2g| Sodium 1419mg | Carbs 0g | Fiber 0g| Sugar 0g | Protein137.5 g

Beef & Broccoli

Servings: 4 | Cooking Time: 12

Ingredients:
- 12 ounces of teriyaki sauce, divided
- ½ tablespoon garlic powder
- ¼ cup of soy sauce
- 1 pound raw sirloin steak, thinly sliced
- 2 cups broccoli, cut into florets
- 2 teaspoons of olive oil
- Salt and black pepper, to taste

Directions:
1. Take a zip-lock plastic bag and mix teriyaki sauce, salt, garlic powder, black pepper, soy sauce, and olive oil.
2. Marinate the beef in it for 2 hours.
3. Then drain the beef from the marinade.
4. Now toss the broccoli with oil, teriyaki sauce, and salt and black pepper.
5. Put it in a zone 1 basket
6. Now for the zone, 1 basket set it to AIRFRY mode at 400 degrees F for 15 minutes.
7. Place the steak in a zone 2 basket and set it to AIR FRY mode at 375 degrees F for 10-12 minutes.
8. Hit start and let the cooking cycle completes.
9. Once it's done take out the beef and broccoli and
10. serve immediately with leftover teriyaki sauce and cooked rice.

Nutrition Info:
- (Per serving) Calories 344| Fat 10g| Sodium 4285mg | Carbs18.2 g | Fiber 1.5g| Sugar 13.3g | Protein42 g

Meatballs

Servings: 4 | Cooking Time: 20 Minutes

Ingredients:
- 450g ground beef
- 59ml milk
- 45g parmesan cheese, grated
- 50g breadcrumbs
- ½ tsp Italian seasoning
- 2 garlic cloves, minced
- Pepper
- Salt

Directions:
1. In a bowl, mix the meat and remaining ingredients until well combined.
2. Insert a crisper plate in the Ninja Foodi air fryer baskets.
3. Make small balls from the meat mixture and place them in both baskets.
4. Select zone 1, then select "air fry" mode and set the temperature to 375 degrees F for 15 minutes. Press "match" and "start/stop" to begin.

Nutrition Info:
- (Per serving) Calories 426 | Fat 17.3g |Sodium 820mg | Carbs 11.1g | Fiber 0.7g | Sugar 1.6g | Protein 48.8g

Curry-crusted Lamb Chops With Baked Brown Sugar Acorn Squash

Servings:4 | Cooking Time: 20 Minutes

Ingredients:

- FOR THE LAMB CHOPS
- 4 lamb loin chops (4 ounces each)
- 1 tablespoon olive oil
- 2 teaspoons curry powder
- ¼ teaspoon kosher salt

- FOR THE ACORN SQUASH
- 2 small acorn squash
- 4 teaspoons dark brown sugar
- 2 teaspoons salted butter
- ⅛ teaspoon kosher salt

Directions:

1. To prep the lamb chops: Brush both sides of the lamb chops with the oil and season with the curry powder and salt.
2. To prep the acorn squash: Cut the squash in half through the stem end and remove the seeds. Place 1 teaspoon of brown sugar and ½ teaspoon of butter into the well of each squash half.
3. To cook the lamb and squash: Install a crisper plate in each of the two baskets. Place the lamb chops in the Zone 1 basket and insert the basket in the unit. Place the squash cut-side up in the Zone 2 basket and insert the basket in the unit.
4. Select Zone 1, select AIR FRY, set the temperature to 400°F, and set the timer to 15 minutes.
5. Select Zone 2, select BAKE, set the temperature to 400°F, and set the time to 20 minutes. Select SMART FINISH.
6. Press START/PAUSE to begin cooking.
7. When both timers read 5 minutes, press START/PAUSE. Remove the Zone 1 basket and use a pair of silicone-tipped tongs to flip the lamb chops. Reinsert the basket in the unit. Remove the Zone 2 basket and spoon the melted butter and sugar over the top edges of the squash. Reinsert the basket and press START/PAUSE to resume cooking.
8. When cooking is complete, the lamb should be cooked to your liking and the squash soft when pierced with a fork.
9. Remove the lamb chops from the basket and let rest for 5 minutes. Season the acorn squash with salt before serving.

Nutrition Info:

- (Per serving) Calories: 328; Total fat: 19g; Saturated fat: 7.5g; Carbohydrates: 23g; Fiber: 3g; Protein: 16g; Sodium: 172mg

Italian Sausages With Peppers, Potatoes, And Onions

Servings:4 | Cooking Time: 22 Minutes

Ingredients:

- FOR THE PEPPERS, POTATOES, AND ONIONS
- 2 Yukon Gold potatoes, cut into ¼-inch slices
- 1 red bell pepper, sliced
- 1 yellow onion, sliced
- ¼ cup canned tomato sauce
- 1 tablespoon olive oil
- 1 teaspoon minced garlic
- ½ teaspoon dried oregano
- ¼ teaspoon kosher salt
- FOR THE SAUSAGES
- 4 links Italian sausage

Directions:

1. To prep the peppers, potatoes, and onions: In a large bowl, combine the potatoes, pepper, onion, tomato sauce, oil, garlic, oregano, and salt. Mix to combine.
2. To cook the sausage and vegetables: Install a crisper plate in each of the two baskets. Place the sausages in the Zone 1 basket and insert the basket in the unit. Place the potato mixture in the Zone 2 basket and insert the basket in the unit.
3. Select Zone 1, select AIR FRY, set the temperature to 390°F, and set the time to 22 minutes.
4. Select Zone 2, select ROAST, set the temperature to 375°F, and set the time to 20 minutes. Select SMART FINISH.
5. Press START/PAUSE to begin cooking.
6. When cooking is complete, the sausages will be cooked through and the vegetables tender.
7. Slice the sausages into rounds, then mix them into the potato and pepper mixture. Serve.

Nutrition Info:

- (Per serving) Calories: 335; Total fat: 22g; Saturated fat: 6.5g; Carbohydrates: 21g; Fiber: 2g; Protein: 15g; Sodium: 658mg

Pork With Green Beans And Potatoes

Servings: 4 | Cooking Time: 15 Minutes.

Ingredients:
- ¼ cup Dijon mustard
- 2 tablespoons brown sugar
- 1 teaspoon dried parsley flake
- ½ teaspoon dried thyme
- ¼ teaspoons salt
- ¼ teaspoons black pepper
- 1 ¼ lbs. pork tenderloin
- ¾ lb. small potatoes halved
- 1 (12-oz) package green beans, trimmed
- 1 tablespoon olive oil
- Salt and black pepper ground to taste

Directions:
1. Preheat your Air Fryer Machine to 400 degrees F.
2. Add mustard, parsley, brown sugar, salt, black pepper, and thyme in a large bowl, then mix well.
3. Add tenderloin to the spice mixture and coat well.
4. Toss potatoes with olive oil, salt, black pepper, and green beans in another bowl.
5. Place the prepared tenderloin in the crisper plate.
6. Return this crisper plate to the Zone 1 of the Ninja Foodi Dual Zone Air Fryer.
7. Choose the Air Fry mode for Zone 1 and set the temperature to 390 degrees F and the time to 15 minutes.
8. Add potatoes and green beans to the Zone 2.
9. Choose the Air Fry mode for Zone 2 with 350 degrees F and the time to 10 minutes.
10. Press the SYNC button to sync the finish time for both Zones.
11. Initiate cooking by pressing the START/STOP button.
12. Serve the tenderloin with Air Fried potatoes

Nutrition Info:
- (Per serving) Calories 400 | Fat 32g |Sodium 721mg | Carbs 2.6g | Fiber 0g | Sugar 0g | Protein 27.4g

Glazed Steak Recipe

Servings:2 | Cooking Time:25

Ingredients:
- 1 pound of beef steaks
- ½ cup, soy sauce
- Salt and black pepper, to taste
- 1 tablespoon of vegetable oil
- 1 teaspoon of grated ginger
- 4 cloves garlic, minced
- 1/4 cup brown sugar

Directions:
1. Take a bowl and whisk together soy sauce, salt, pepper, vegetable oil, garlic, brown sugar, and ginger.
2. Once a paste is made rub the steak with the marinate
3. Let it sit for 30 minutes.
4. After 30 minutes add the steak to the air fryer basket and set it to AIR BROIL mode at 400 degrees F for 18-22 minutes.
5. After 10 minutes, hit pause and takeout the basket.
6. Let the steak flip and again let it AIR BROIL for the remaining minutes.
7. Once 25 minutes of cooking cycle completes.
8. Take out the steak and let it rest. Serve by cutting into slices.
9. Enjoy.

Nutrition Info:
- (Per serving) Calories 563| Fat 21 g| Sodium 156mg | Carbs 20.6g | Fiber0.3 g| Sugar17.8 g | Protein69.4 g

Short Ribs & Root Vegetables

Servings: 2 | Cooking Time: 45

Ingredients:

- 1 pound of beef short ribs, bone-in and trimmed
- Salt and black pepper, to taste
- 2 tablespoons canola oil, divided
- 1/4 cup red wine
- 3 tablespoons brown sugar
- 2 cloves garlic, peeled, minced
- 4 carrots, peeled, cut into 1-inch pieces
- 2 parsnips, peeled, cut into 1-inch pieces
- ½ cup pearl onions

Directions:

1. Season the ribs with salt and black pepper and rub a little amount of canola oil on both sides.
2. Place it in zone 1 basket of the air fryer.
3. Next, take a bowl and add pearl onions, parsnip, carrots, garlic, brown sugar, red wine, salt, and black pepper.
4. Add the vegetable mixture to the zone 2 basket.
5. Set the zone 1 basket time to 12 minutes at 375 degrees F at AIR FRY mode.
6. Set the zone 2 basket at AIR FRY mode at 390 degrees F for 18 minutes.
7. Hit start so the cooking cycle being.
8. Once the cooking complete, take out the ingredient and serve short ribs with the mixed vegetables and liquid collect at the bottom of zone 2 basket
9. Enjoy it hot.

Nutrition Info:

- (Per serving) Calories1262 | Fat 98.6g| Sodium 595mg | Carbs 57g | Fiber 10.1g| Sugar 28.2g | Protein 35.8g

Italian-style Meatballs With Garlicky Roasted Broccoli

Servings: 4 | Cooking Time: 15 Minutes

Ingredients:

- FOR THE MEATBALLS
- 1 large egg
- ¼ cup Italian-style bread crumbs
- 1 pound ground beef (85 percent lean)
- ¼ cup grated Parmesan cheese
- ¼ teaspoon kosher salt
- Nonstick cooking spray
- 2 cups marinara sauce
- FOR THE ROASTED BROCCOLI
- 4 cups broccoli florets
- 1 tablespoon olive oil
- ¼ teaspoon kosher salt
- ¼ teaspoon freshly ground pepper
- ¼ teaspoon red pepper flakes
- 1 tablespoon minced garlic

Directions:

1. To prep the meatballs: In a large bowl, beat the egg. Mix in the bread crumbs and let sit for 5 minutes.
2. Add the beef, Parmesan, and salt and mix until just combined. Form the meatball mixture into 8 meatballs, about 1 inch in diameter. Mist with cooking spray.
3. To prep the broccoli: In a large bowl, combine the broccoli, olive oil, salt, black pepper, and red pepper flakes. Toss to coat the broccoli evenly.
4. To cook the meatballs and broccoli: Install a crisper plate in the Zone 1 basket. Place the meatballs in the basket and insert the basket in the unit. Place the broccoli in the Zone 2 basket, sprinkle the garlic over the broccoli, and insert the basket in the unit.
5. Select Zone 1, select AIR FRY, set the temperature to 400°F, and set the time to 12 minutes.
6. Select Zone 2, select ROAST, set the temperature to 390°F, and set the time to 15 minutes. Select SMART FINISH.
7. Press START/PAUSE to begin cooking.
8. When the Zone 1 timer reads 5 minutes, press START/PAUSE. Remove the basket and pour the marinara sauce over the meatballs. Reinsert the basket and press START/PAUSE to resume cooking.
9. When cooking is complete, the meatballs should be cooked through and the broccoli will have begun to brown on the edges.

Nutrition Info:

- (Per serving) Calories: 493; Total fat: 33g; Saturated fat: 9g; Carbohydrates: 24g; Fiber: 3g; Protein: 31g; Sodium: 926mg

Mustard Rubbed Lamb Chops

Servings: 4 | Cooking Time: 31 Minutes.

Ingredients:
- 1 teaspoon Dijon mustard
- 1 teaspoon olive oil
- ½ teaspoon soy sauce
- ½ teaspoon garlic, minced
- ½ teaspoon cumin powder
- ½ teaspoon cayenne pepper
- ½ teaspoon Italian spice blend
- ⅛ teaspoon salt
- 4 pieces of lamb chops

Directions:
1. Mix Dijon mustard, soy sauce, olive oil, garlic, cumin powder, cayenne pepper, Italian spice blend, and salt in a medium bowl and mix well.
2. Place lamb chops into a Ziploc bag and pour in the marinade.
3. Press the air out of the bag and seal tightly.
4. Press the marinade around the lamb chops to coat.
5. Keep then in the fridge and marinate for at least 30 minutes, up to overnight.
6. Place 2 chops in each of the crisper plate and spray them with cooking oil.
7. Return the crisper plate to the Ninja Foodi Dual Zone Air Fryer.
8. Select the Roast mode for Zone 1 and set the temperature to 350 degrees F and the time to 27 minutes.
9. Select the "MATCH" button to copy the settings for Zone 2.
10. Initiate cooking by pressing the START/STOP button.
11. Flip the chops once cooked halfway through, and resume cooking.
12. Switch the Roast mode to Max Crisp mode and cook for 5 minutes.
13. Serve warm.

Nutrition Info:
- (Per serving) Calories 264 | Fat 17g | Sodium 129mg | Carbs 0.9g | Fiber 0.3g | Sugar 0g | Protein 27g

Beef Kofta Kebab

Servings: 4 | Cooking Time: 18 Minutes

Ingredients:
- 455g ground beef
- ¼ cup white onion, grated
- ¼ cup parsley, chopped
- 1 tablespoon mint, chopped
- 2 cloves garlic, minced
- 1 teaspoon salt
- ½ teaspoon cumin
- 1 teaspoon oregano
- ½ teaspoon garlic salt
- 1 egg

Directions:
1. Mix ground beef with onion, parsley, mint, garlic, cumin, oregano, garlic salt and egg in a bowl.
2. Take 3 tbsp-sized beef kebabs out of this mixture.
3. Place the kebabs in the air fryer baskets.
4. Return the air fryer basket 1 to Zone 1, and basket 2 to Zone 2 of the Ninja Foodi 2-Basket Air Fryer.
5. Choose the "Air Fry" mode for Zone 1 at 375 degrees F and 18 minutes of cooking time.
6. Select the "MATCH COOK" option to copy the settings for Zone 2.
7. Initiate cooking by pressing the START/PAUSE BUTTON.
8. Flip the kebabs once cooked halfway through.
9. Serve warm.

Nutrition Info:
- (Per serving) Calories 316 | Fat 12.2g | Sodium 587mg | Carbs 12.2g | Fiber 1g | Sugar 1.8g | Protein 25.8g

Marinated Pork Chops

Servings: 2 | Cooking Time: 12 Minutes

Ingredients:
- 2 pork chops, boneless
- 18g sugar
- 1 tbsp water
- 15ml rice wine
- 15ml dark soy sauce
- 15ml light soy sauce
- ½ tsp cinnamon
- ½ tsp five-spice powder
- 1 tsp black pepper

Directions:
1. Add pork chops and remaining ingredients into a zip-lock bag. Seal the bag and place in the refrigerator for 4 hours.
2. Insert a crisper plate in the Ninja Foodi air fryer baskets.
3. Place the marinated pork chops in both baskets.
4. Select zone 1, then select air fry mode and set the temperature to 380 degrees F for 12 minutes. Press "match" to match zone 2 settings to zone 1. Press "start/stop" to begin.

Nutrition Info:
- (Per serving) Calories 306 | Fat 19.9g | Sodium 122mg | Carbs 13.7g | Fiber 0.6g | Sugar 11g | Protein 18.1g

Lamb Chops With Dijon Garlic

Servings: 4 | Cooking Time: 22 Minutes

Ingredients:
- 2 teaspoons Dijon mustard
- 2 teaspoons olive oil
- 1 teaspoon soy sauce
- 1 teaspoon garlic, minced
- 1 teaspoon cumin powder
- 1 teaspoon cayenne pepper
- 1 teaspoon Italian spice blend (optional)
- ¼ teaspoon salt
- 8 lamb chops

Directions:
1. Combine the Dijon mustard, olive oil, soy sauce, garlic, cumin powder, cayenne pepper, Italian spice blend (optional), and salt in a medium mixing bowl.
2. Put the marinade in a large Ziploc bag. Add the lamb chops. Seal the bag tightly after pressing out the air. Coat the lamb in the marinade by shaking the bag and pressing the chops into the mixture. Place in the fridge for at least 30 minutes, or up to overnight, to marinate.
3. Install a crisper plate in both drawers. Place half the lamb chops in the zone 1 drawer and half in zone 2's, then insert the drawers into the unit.
4. Select zone 1, select AIR FRY, set temperature to 390 degrees F/ 200 degrees C, and set time to 22 minutes. Select MATCH to match zone 2 settings to zone 1. Press the START/STOP button to begin cooking.
5. When the time reaches 11 minutes, press START/STOP to pause the unit. Remove the drawers and flip the lamb chops. Re-insert the drawers into the unit and press START/STOP to resume cooking.
6. Serve and enjoy!

Nutrition Info:
- (Per serving) Calories 343 | Fat 15.1g | Sodium 380mg | Carbs 0.9 g | Fiber 0.3g | Sugar 0.1g | Protein 48.9g

Chinese Bbq Pork

Servings:35 | Cooking Time:25

Ingredients:
- 4 tablespoons of soy sauce
- ¼ cup red wine
- 2 tablespoons of oyster sauce
- ¼ tablespoons of hoisin sauce
- ¼ cup honey
- ¼ cup brown sugar
- Pinch of salt
- Pinch of black pepper
- 1 teaspoon of ginger garlic, paste
- 1 teaspoon of five-spice powder
- 1.5 pounds of pork shoulder, sliced

Directions:
1. Take a bowl and mix all the ingredients listed under sauce ingredients.
2. Transfer half of it to a sauce pan and let it cook for 10 minutes.
3. Set it aside.
4. Let the pork marinate in the remaining sauce for 2 hours.
5. Afterward, put the pork slices in the basket and set it to AIRBORIL mode 450 degrees for 25 minutes.
6. Make sure the internal temperature is above 160 degrees F once cooked.
7. If not add a few more minutes to the overall cooking time.
8. Once done, take it out and baste it with prepared sauce.
9. Serve and Enjoy.

Nutrition Info:
- (Per serving) Calories 1239| Fat 73 g| Sodium 2185 mg | Carbs 57.3 g | Fiber 0.4g| Sugar53.7 g | Protein 81.5 g

Marinated Steak & Mushrooms

Servings: 4 | Cooking Time: 10 Minutes

Ingredients:
- 450g rib-eye steak, cut into ½-inch pieces
- 2 tsp dark soy sauce
- 2 tsp light soy sauce
- 15ml lime juice
- 15ml rice wine
- 15ml oyster sauce
- 1 tbsp garlic, chopped
- 8 mushrooms, sliced
- 2 tbsp ginger, grated
- 1 tsp cornstarch
- ¼ tsp pepper

Directions:
1. Add steak pieces, mushrooms, and the remaining ingredients to a zip-lock bag. Seal the bag and place it in the refrigerator for 2 hours.
2. Insert a crisper plate in the Ninja Foodi air fryer baskets.
3. Remove the steak pieces and mushrooms from the marinade and place them in both baskets.
4. Select zone 1, then select "air fry" mode and set the temperature to 380 degrees F for 10 minutes. Press "match" to match zone 2 settings to zone 1. Press "start/stop" to begin. Stir halfway through.

Nutrition Info:
- (Per serving) Calories 341 | Fat 25.4g |Sodium 128mg | Carbs 6.3g | Fiber 0.8g | Sugar 1.7g | Protein 21.6g

Poultry Recipes

Bacon Wrapped Stuffed Chicken 37
Juicy Duck Breast 37
Lemon Chicken Thighs 38
Sesame Ginger Chicken 38
Almond Chicken 39
Pretzel Chicken Cordon Bleu 39
Crispy Sesame Chicken 40
Chicken Parmesan 40
Orange Chicken With Roasted Snap Peas And Scallions . 41
Chicken Tenders And Curly Fries 42
Sweet And Spicy Carrots With Chicken Thighs 42
Chicken Potatoes 43
Balsamic Duck Breast 43
Spicy Chicken Wings 44
Thai Curry Chicken Kabobs 44

Poultry Recipes

Bacon Wrapped Stuffed Chicken

Servings: 4 | Cooking Time: 25 Minutes

Ingredients:
- 3 boneless chicken breasts
- 6 jalapenos, sliced
- ¾ cup (170g) cream cheese
- ½ cup Monterey Jack cheese, shredded
- 1 teaspoon ground cumin
- 12 strips thick bacon

Directions:
1. Cut the chicken breasts in half crosswise and pound them with a mallet.
2. Mix cream cheese with cumin and Monterey jacket cheese in a bowl.
3. Spread the cream cheese mixture over the chicken breast slices.
4. Add jalapeno slices on top and wrap the chicken slices.
5. Wrap each chicken rolls with a bacon slice.
6. Place the wrapped rolls into the Ninja Foodi 2 Baskets Air Fryer baskets.
7. Return the air fryer basket 1 to Zone 1, and basket 2 to Zone 2 of the Ninja Foodi 2-Basket Air Fryer.
8. Choose the "Air Fry" mode for Zone 1 at 340 degrees F and 25 minutes of cooking time.
9. Select the "MATCH COOK" option to copy the settings for Zone 2.
10. Initiate cooking by pressing the START/PAUSE BUTTON.
11. Serve warm.

Nutrition Info:
- (Per serving) Calories 220 | Fat 1.7g | Sodium 178mg | Carbs 1.7g | Fiber 0.2g | Sugar 0.2g | Protein 32.9g

Juicy Duck Breast

Servings: 1 | Cooking Time: 20 Minutes

Ingredients:
- ½ duck breast
- Salt and black pepper, to taste
- 2 tablespoons plum sauce

Directions:
1. Rub the duck breast with black pepper and salt.
2. Place the duck breast in air fryer basket 1 and add plum sauce on top.
3. Return the basket to the Ninja Foodi 2 Baskets Air Fryer.
4. Choose the "Air Fry" mode for Zone 1 and set the temperature to 400 degrees F and 20 minutes of cooking time.
5. Initiate cooking by pressing the START/PAUSE BUTTON.
6. Flip the duck breast once cooked halfway through.
7. Serve warm.

Nutrition Info:
- (Per serving) Calories 379 | Fat 19g | Sodium 184mg | Carbs 12.3g | Fiber 0.6g | Sugar 2g | Protein 37.7g

Lemon Chicken Thighs

Servings: 4 | Cooking Time: 25 Minutes

Ingredients:
- ¼ cup butter, softened
- 3 garlic cloves, minced
- 2 teaspoons minced fresh rosemary or ½ teaspoon crushed dried rosemary
- 1 teaspoon minced fresh thyme or ¼ teaspoon dried thyme
- 1 teaspoon grated lemon zest
- 1 tablespoon lemon juice
- 4 bone-in chicken thighs (about 1½ pounds)
- 1/8 teaspoon salt
- 1/8 teaspoon pepper

Directions:
1. Combine the butter, garlic, rosemary, thyme, lemon zest, and lemon juice in a small bowl.
2. Under the skin of each chicken thigh, spread 1 teaspoon of the butter mixture. Apply the remaining butter to each thigh's skin. Season to taste with salt and pepper.
3. Install a crisper plate in both drawers. Place half the chicken tenders in the zone 1 drawer and half in zone 2's, then insert the drawers into the unit.
4. Select zone 1, select AIR FRY, set temperature to 390 degrees F/ 200 degrees C, and set time to 22 minutes. Select MATCH to match zone 2 settings to zone 1. Press the START/STOP button to begin cooking.
5. When the time reaches 11 minutes, press START/STOP to pause the unit. Remove the drawers and flip the chicken. Re-insert the drawers into the unit and press START/STOP to resume cooking.
6. When cooking is complete, remove the chicken and serve.

Nutrition Info:
- (Per serving) Calories 329 | Fat 26g | Sodium 253mg | Carbs 1g | Fiber 0g | Sugar 0g | Protein 23g

Sesame Ginger Chicken

Servings: 4 | Cooking Time: 30 Minutes

Ingredients:
- 4 ounces green beans
- 1 tablespoon canola oil
- 1½ pounds boneless, skinless chicken breasts
- 1/3 cup prepared sesame-ginger sauce
- Kosher salt, to taste
- Black pepper, to taste

Directions:
1. Toss the green beans with a teaspoon of salt and pepper in a medium mixing bowl.
2. Place a crisper plate in each drawer. Place the green beans in the zone 1 drawer and insert it into the unit. Place the chicken breasts in the zone 2 drawer and place it inside the unit.
3. Select zone 1, then AIR FRY, and set the temperature to 390 degrees F/ 200 degrees C with a 10-minute timer. Select zone 2, then AIR FRY, and set the temperature to 390 degrees F/ 200 degrees C with an 18-minute timer. Select SYNC. To begin cooking, press the START/STOP button.
4. Press START/STOP to pause the unit when the zone 2 timer reaches 9 minutes. Remove the chicken from the drawer and toss it in the sesame ginger sauce. To resume cooking, re-insert the drawer into the unit and press START/STOP.
5. When cooking is complete, serve the chicken breasts and green beans straight away.

Nutrition Info:
- (Per serving) Calories 143 | Fat 7g | Sodium 638mg | Carbs 11.6g | Fiber 1.4g | Sugar 8.5g | Protein 11.1g

Almond Chicken

Servings: 4 | Cooking Time: 25 Minutes

Ingredients:
- 2 large eggs
- ½ cup buttermilk
- 2 teaspoons garlic salt
- 1 teaspoon pepper
- 2 cups slivered almonds, finely chopped
- 4 boneless, skinless chicken breast halves (6 ounces each)

Directions:
1. Whisk together the egg, buttermilk, garlic salt, and pepper in a small bowl.
2. In another small bowl, place the almonds.
3. Dip the chicken in the egg mixture, then roll it in the almonds, patting it down to help the coating stick.
4. Install a crisper plate in both drawers. Place half the chicken breasts in the zone 1 drawer and half in zone 2's, then insert the drawers into the unit.
5. Select zone 1, select AIR FRY, set temperature to 390 degrees F/ 200 degrees C, and set time to 22 minutes. Select MATCH to match zone 2 settings to zone 1. Press the START/STOP button to begin cooking.
6. When the time reaches 11 minutes, press START/STOP to pause the unit. Remove the drawers and flip the chicken. Re-insert the drawers into the unit and press START/STOP to resume cooking.
7. When cooking is complete, remove the chicken.

Nutrition Info:
- (Per serving) Calories 353 | Fat 18g | Sodium 230mg | Carbs 6g | Fiber 2g | Sugar 3g | Protein 41g

Pretzel Chicken Cordon Bleu

Servings: 4 | Cooking Time: 26 Minutes

Ingredients:
- 5 boneless chicken thighs
- 3 cups pretzels, crushed
- 2 eggs, beaten
- 10 deli honey ham, slices
- 5 Swiss cheese slices
- Cooking spray

Directions:
1. Grind pretzels in a food processor.
2. Pound the chicken tights with a mallet.
3. Top each chicken piece with one cheese slice and 2 ham slices.
4. Roll the chicken pieces and secure with a toothpick.
5. Dip the rolls in the eggs and coat with the breadcrumbs.
6. Place these rolls in the air fryer baskets.
7. Spray them with cooking oil.
8. Return the air fryer basket 1 to Zone 1, and basket 2 to Zone 2 of the Ninja Foodi 2-Basket Air Fryer.
9. Choose the "Air Fry" mode for Zone 1 and set the temperature to 375 degrees F and 26 minutes of cooking time.
10. Select the "MATCH COOK" option to copy the settings for Zone 2.
11. Initiate cooking by pressing the START/PAUSE BUTTON.
12. Flip the rolls once cooked halfway through.
13. Serve warm.

Nutrition Info:
- (Per serving) Calories 380 | Fat 29g | Sodium 821mg | Carbs 34.6g | Fiber 0g | Sugar 0g | Protein 30g

Crispy Sesame Chicken

Servings: 2 | Cooking Time: 10 Minutes

Ingredients:

- 680g boneless chicken thighs, diced
- 2 tablespoons rice vinegar
- 1 tablespoon soy sauce
- 2 teaspoons minced fresh ginger
- 1 garlic clove, minced
- ¾ teaspoon salt
- ½ teaspoon black pepper
- 2 large eggs, beaten
- 1 cup cornstarch
- Sauce
- 59ml soy sauce
- 2 tablespoons rice vinegar
- ⅓ cup brown sugar
- 59ml water
- 1 tablespoon cornstarch
- 2 teaspoons sesame oil
- 2 tablespoons vegetable oil
- 2 garlic cloves, minced
- 2 teaspoons chile paste
- Garnish
- 1 tablespoon toasted sesame seeds

Directions:

1. Blend all the sauce ingredients in a saucepan and cook until it thickens then allow it to cool.
2. Mix chicken with black pepper, salt, garlic, ginger, vinegar, and soy sauce in a bowl.
3. Cover and marinate the chicken for 20 minutes.
4. Divide the chicken in the air fryer baskets.
5. Return the air fryer basket 1 to Zone 1, and basket 2 to Zone 2 of the Ninja Foodi 2-Basket Air Fryer.
6. Choose the "Air Fry" mode for Zone 1 and set the temperature to 400 degrees F and 10 minutes of cooking time.
7. Select the "MATCH COOK" option to copy the settings for Zone 2.
8. Initiate cooking by pressing the START/PAUSE BUTTON.
9. Pour the prepared sauce over the air fried chicken and drizzle sesame seeds on top.
10. Serve warm.

Nutrition Info:

- (Per serving) Calories 351 | Fat 16g | Sodium 777mg | Carbs 26g | Fiber 4g | Sugar 5g | Protein 28g

Chicken Parmesan

Servings: 4 | Cooking Time: 20 Minutes

Ingredients:

- 2 large eggs
- ½ cup seasoned breadcrumbs
- ⅓ cup grated parmesan cheese
- ¼ teaspoon pepper
- 4 boneless, skinless chicken breast halves (6 ounces each)
- 1 cup pasta sauce
- 1 cup shredded mozzarella cheese
- Chopped fresh basil (optional)

Directions:

1. Lightly beat the eggs in a small bowl.
2. Combine the breadcrumbs, parmesan cheese, and pepper in a shallow bowl.
3. After dipping the chicken in the egg, coat it in the crumb mixture.
4. Install a crisper plate in both drawers. Place half the chicken breasts in the zone 1 drawer and half in zone 2's, then insert the drawers into the unit.
5. Select zone 1, select AIR FRY, set temperature to 390 degrees F/ 200 degrees C, and set time to 20 minutes. Select MATCH to match zone 2 settings to zone 1. Press the START/STOP button to begin cooking.
6. When the time reaches 10 minutes, press START/STOP to pause the unit. Remove the drawers and flip the chicken. Re-insert the drawers into the unit and press START/STOP to resume cooking.
7. When cooking is complete, remove the chicken.

Nutrition Info:

- (Per serving) Calories 293 | Fat 15.8g | Sodium 203mg | Carbs 11.1g | Fiber 2.4g | Sugar 8.7g | Protein 29g

Orange Chicken With Roasted Snap Peas And Scallions

Servings: 4 | Cooking Time: 30 Minutes

Ingredients:
- FOR THE CHICKEN
- ⅓ cup all-purpose flour
- 2 large eggs
- ⅓ cup cornstarch, plus 2 tablespoons
- 1½ pounds boneless, skinless chicken breasts, cut into 1-inch pieces
- Nonstick cooking spray
- 2 tablespoons grated orange zest
- 1 cup freshly squeezed orange juice
- ¼ cup granulated sugar
- 2 tablespoons rice vinegar
- 2 tablespoons soy sauce
- ¼ teaspoon minced fresh ginger
- ¼ teaspoon grated garlic
- FOR THE SNAP PEAS
- 8 ounces snap peas
- 1 tablespoon vegetable oil
- ½ teaspoon minced garlic
- ½ teaspoon grated fresh ginger
- ¼ teaspoon kosher salt
- ¼ teaspoon freshly ground black pepper
- 4 scallions, thinly sliced

Directions:

1. To prep the chicken: Set up a breading station with three small shallow bowls. Place the flour in the first bowl. In the second bowl, beat the eggs. Place ⅓ cup of cornstarch in the third bowl.
2. Bread the chicken pieces in this order: First, dip them into the flour to coat. Then, dip into the beaten egg. Finally, add them to the cornstarch, coating all sides. Mist the breaded chicken with cooking spray.
3. In a small bowl, whisk together the orange zest, orange juice, sugar, vinegar, soy sauce, ginger, garlic, and remaining 2 tablespoons of cornstarch. Set orange sauce aside.
4. To prep the snap peas: In a large bowl, combine the snap peas, oil, garlic, ginger, salt, and black pepper. Toss to coat.
5. To cook the chicken and snap peas: Install a crisper plate in the Zone 1 basket. Add the chicken to the basket and insert the basket in the unit. Place the snap peas in the Zone 2 basket and insert the basket in the unit.
6. Select Zone 1, select AIR FRY, set the temperature to 400°F, and set the time to 30 minutes.
7. Select Zone 2, select ROAST, set the temperature to 375°F, and set the time to 12 minutes. Select SMART FINISH.
8. Press START/PAUSE to begin cooking.
9. When the Zone 1 timer reads 15 minutes, press START/PAUSE. Remove the basket and shake to redistribute the chicken. Reinsert the basket and press START/PAUSE to resume cooking.
10. When the Zone 1 timer reads 5 minutes, press START/PAUSE. Remove the basket and pour the reserved orange sauce over the chicken. Reinsert the basket and press START/PAUSE to resume cooking.
11. When cooking is complete, the chicken and vegetables will be cooked through. Stir the scallions into the snap peas. Serve hot.

Nutrition Info:
- (Per serving) Calories: 473; Total fat: 13g; Saturated fat: 2g; Carbohydrates: 43g; Fiber: 2g; Protein: 44g; Sodium: 803mg

Chicken Tenders And Curly Fries

Servings: 4 | Cooking Time: 35 Minutes

Ingredients:
- 1-pound frozen chicken tenders
- 1-pound frozen curly French fries
- Dipping sauces of your choice

Directions:
1. Place a crisper plate in each drawer. In the zone 1 drawer, place the chicken tenders, then place the drawer into the unit.
2. Fill the zone 2 drawer with the curly French fries, then place the drawer in the unit.
3. Select zone 1, then AIR FRY, and set the temperature to 390 degrees F/ 200 degrees C with a 22-minute timer. Select zone 2, then AIR FRY, and set the temperature to 400 degrees F/ 200 degrees C with a 30-minute timer. Select SYNC. To begin cooking, press the START/STOP button.
4. Press START/STOP to pause the device when the zone 1 and 2 times reach 8 minutes. Shake the drawers for 10 seconds after removing them from the unit. To resume cooking, re-insert the drawers into the unit and press START/STOP.
5. Enjoy!

Nutrition Info:
- (Per serving) Calories 500 | Fat 19.8g | Sodium 680mg | Carbs 50.1g | Fiber 4.1g | Sugar 0g | Protein 27.9g

Sweet And Spicy Carrots With Chicken Thighs

Servings:2 | Cooking Time:35

Ingredients:
- Cooking spray, for greasing
- 2 tablespoons butter, melted
- 1 tablespoon hot honey
- 1 teaspoon orange zest
- 1 teaspoon cardamom
- ½ pound baby carrots
- 1 tablespoon orange juice
- Salt and black pepper, to taste
- ½ pound of carrots, baby carrots
- 8 chicken thighs

Directions:
1. Take a bowl and mix all the glaze ingredients in it.
2. Now, coat the chicken and carrots with the glaze and let it rest for 30 minutes.
3. Now place the chicken thighs into the zone 1 basket.
4. Next put the glazed carrots into the zone 2 basket.
5. Press button 1 for the first basket and set it to ROAST Mode at 350 degrees F for 35 minutes.
6. For the second basket hit 2 and set time to AIRFRY mode at 390 degrees F for 8-10 minutes.
7. Once the cooking cycle completes take out the carrots and chicken and serve it hot.

Nutrition Info:
- (Per serving) Calories 1312| Fat 55.4g| Sodium 757mg | Carbs 23.3g | Fiber6.7 g | Sugar12 g | Protein171 g

Chicken Potatoes

Servings: 4 | Cooking Time: 22 Minutes.

Ingredients:
- 15 ounces canned potatoes drained
- 1 teaspoon olive oil
- 1 teaspoon Lawry's seasoned salt
- ⅛ teaspoons black pepper optional
- 8 ounces boneless chicken breast cubed
- ¼ teaspoon paprika
- ⅜ cup cheddar, shredded
- 4 bacon slices, cooked, cut into strips

Directions:
1. Dice the chicken into small pieces and toss them with olive oil and spices.
2. Drain and dice the potato pieces into smaller cubes.
3. Add potato to the chicken and mix well to coat.
4. Spread the mixture in the two crisper plates in a single layer.
5. Return the crisper plates to the Ninja Foodi Dual Zone Air Fryer.
6. Choose the Air Fry mode for Zone 1 and set the temperature to 390 degrees F and the time to 22 minutes.
7. Select the "MATCH" button to copy the settings for Zone 2.
8. Initiate cooking by pressing the START/STOP button.
9. Top the chicken and potatoes with cheese and bacon.
10. Return the crisper plates to the Ninja Foodi Dual Zone Air Fryer.
11. Select the Max Crisp mode for Zone 1 and set the temperature to 300 degrees F and the time to 5 minutes.
12. Initiate cooking by pressing the START/STOP button.
13. Repeat the same step for Zone 2 to broil the potatoes and chicken in the right drawer.
14. Enjoy with dried herbs on top.

Nutrition Info:
- (Per serving) Calories 346 | Fat 16.1g | Sodium 882mg | Carbs 1.3g | Fiber 0.5g | Sugar 0.5g | Protein 48.2g

Balsamic Duck Breast

Servings: 2 | Cooking Time: 20 Minutes.

Ingredients:
- 2 duck breasts
- 1 teaspoon parsley
- Salt and black pepper, to taste
- Marinade:
- 1 tablespoon olive oil
- ½ teaspoon French mustard
- 1 teaspoon dried garlic
- 2 teaspoons honey
- ½ teaspoon balsamic vinegar

Directions:
1. Mix olive oil, mustard, garlic, honey, and balsamic vinegar in a bowl.
2. Add duck breasts to the marinade and rub well.
3. Place one duck breast in each crisper plate.
4. Return the crisper plates to the Ninja Foodi Dual Zone Air Fryer.
5. Choose the Air Fry mode for Zone 1 and set the temperature to 360 degrees F and the time to 20 minutes.
6. Select the "MATCH" button to copy the settings for Zone 2.
7. Initiate cooking by pressing the START/STOP button.
8. Flip the duck breasts once cooked halfway through, then resume cooking.
9. Serve warm.

Nutrition Info:
- (Per serving) Calories 546 | Fat 33.1g | Sodium 1201mg | Carbs 30g | Fiber 2.4g | Sugar 9.7g | Protein 32g

Spicy Chicken Wings

Servings: 8 | Cooking Time: 30 Minutes

Ingredients:
- 900g chicken wings
- 1 tsp black pepper
- 12g brown sugar
- 1 tbsp chilli powder
- 57g butter, melted
- 1 tsp smoked paprika
- 1 tsp garlic powder
- 1 tsp salt

Directions:
1. In a bowl, toss chicken wings with remaining ingredients until well coated.
2. Insert a crisper plate in the Ninja Foodi air fryer baskets.
3. Add the chicken wings to both baskets.
4. Select zone 1, then select "air fry" mode and set the temperature to 355 degrees F for 30 minutes. Press "match" to match zone 2 settings to zone 1. Press "start/stop" to begin. Turn halfway through.

Nutrition Info:
- (Per serving) Calories 276 | Fat 14.4g | Sodium 439mg | Carbs 2.2g | Fiber 0.5g | Sugar 1.3g | Protein 33.1g

Thai Curry Chicken Kabobs

Servings: 4 | Cooking Time: 15 Minutes

Ingredients:
- 900g skinless chicken thighs
- 120ml Tamari
- 60ml coconut milk
- 3 tablespoons lime juice
- 3 tablespoons maple syrup
- 2 tablespoons Thai red curry

Directions:
1. Mix red curry paste, honey, lime juice, coconut milk, soy sauce in a bowl.
2. Add this sauce and chicken to a Ziplock bag.
3. Seal the bag and shake it to coat well.
4. Refrigerate the chicken for 2 hours then thread the chicken over wooden skewers.
5. Divide the skewers in the air fryer baskets.
6. Return the air fryer basket 1 to Zone 1, and basket 2 to Zone 2 of the Ninja Foodi 2-Basket Air Fryer.
7. Choose the "Air Fry" mode for Zone 1 at 350 degrees F and 15 minutes of cooking time.
8. Select the "MATCH COOK" option to copy the settings for Zone 2.
9. Initiate cooking by pressing the START/PAUSE BUTTON.
10. Flip the skewers once cooked halfway through.
11. Serve warm.

Nutrition Info:
- (Per serving) Calories 353 | Fat 5g | Sodium 818mg | Carbs 53.2g | Fiber 4.4g | Sugar 8g | Protein 17.3g

Fish And Seafood Recipes

Seafood Shrimp Omelet 46
Tasty Parmesan Shrimp 46
Smoked Salmon 47
Delicious Haddock 47
Roasted Salmon And Parmesan Asparagus 48
Crispy Catfish 48
Broiled Teriyaki Salmon With Eggplant In Stir-fry Sauce ... 49
Furikake Salmon 49
Fish Sandwich 50
Fried Tilapia 50
Tilapia With Mojo And Crispy Plantains 51
Salmon Nuggets 52
Bacon-wrapped Shrimp 52
Shrimp Po'boys With Sweet Potato Fries 53
Glazed Scallops 53

Fish And Seafood Recipes

Seafood Shrimp Omelet

Servings:2 | Cooking Time:15

Ingredients:
- 6 large shrimp, shells removed and chopped
- 6 eggs, beaten
- ½ tablespoon of butter, melted
- 2 tablespoons green onions, sliced
- 1/3 cup of mushrooms, chopped
- 1 pinch paprika
- Salt and black pepper, to taste
- Oil spray, for greasing

Directions:
1. In a large bowl whisk the eggs and add chopped shrimp, butter, green onions, mushrooms, paprika, salt, and black pepper.
2. Take two cake pans that fit inside the air fryer and grease them with oil spray.
3. Pour the egg mixture between the cake pans and place it in two baskets of the air fryer.
4. Turn on the BAKE function of zone 1, and let it cook for 15 minutes at 320 degrees F.
5. Select the MATCH button to match the cooking time for the zone 2 basket.
6. Once the cooking cycle completes, take out, and serve hot.

Nutrition Info:
- (Per serving) Calories 300 | Fat 17.5g | Sodium 368mg | Carbs 2.9g | Fiber 0.3g | Sugar 1.4 g | Protein 32.2 g

Tasty Parmesan Shrimp

Servings: 6 | Cooking Time: 10minutes

Ingredients:
- 908g cooked shrimp, peeled & deveined
- ½ tsp oregano
- 59g parmesan cheese, grated
- 1 tbsp garlic, minced
- 30ml olive oil
- 1 tsp onion powder
- 1 tsp basil
- Pepper
- Salt

Directions:
1. Toss shrimp with oregano, cheese, garlic, oil, onion powder, basil, pepper, and salt in a bowl.
2. Insert a crisper plate in the Ninja Foodi air fryer baskets.
3. Add the shrimp mixture to both baskets.
4. Select zone 1, then select "air fry" mode and set the temperature to 360 degrees F for 10 minutes. Press "match" to match zone 2 settings to zone 1. Press "start/stop" to begin.

Nutrition Info:
- (Per serving) Calories 224 | Fat 7.3g | Sodium 397mg | Carbs 3.2g | Fiber 0.1g | Sugar 0.2g | Protein 34.6g

Smoked Salmon

Servings: 4 | Cooking Time: 12

Ingredients:
- 2 pounds of salmon fillets, smoked
- 6 ounces cream cheese
- 4 tablespoons mayonnaise
- 2 teaspoons of chives, fresh
- 1 teaspoon of lemon zest
- Salt and freshly ground black pepper, to taste
- 2 tablespoons of butter

Directions:
1. Cut the salmon into very small and uniform bite-size pieces.
2. Mix cream cheese, chives, mayonnaise, black pepper, and lemon zest, in a small mixing bowl.
3. Let it sit aside for further use.
4. Coat the salmon pieces with salt and butter.
5. Divide the bite-size pieces into both zones of the air fryer.
6. Set it on AIRFRY mode at 400 degrees F for 12 minutes.
7. Select MATCH for zone 2 basket.
8. Hit start, so the cooking start.
9. Once the salmon is done, top it with a bowl creamy mixture and serve.
10. Enjoy hot.

Nutrition Info:
- (Per serving) Calories 557| Fat 15.7 g| Sodium 371mg | Carbs 4.8 g | Fiber 0g | Sugar 1.1g | Protein 48 g

Delicious Haddock

Servings: 4 | Cooking Time: 10 Minutes

Ingredients:
- 1 egg
- 455g haddock fillets
- 1 tsp seafood seasoning
- 136g flour
- 15ml olive oil
- 119g breadcrumbs
- Pepper
- Salt

Directions:
1. In a shallow dish, whisk egg. Add flour to a plate.
2. In a separate shallow dish, mix breadcrumbs, pepper, seafood seasoning, and salt.
3. Brush fish fillets with oil.
4. Coat each fish fillet with flour, then dip in egg and finally coat with breadcrumbs.
5. Insert a crisper plate in the Ninja Foodi air fryer baskets.
6. Place coated fish fillets in both baskets.
7. Select zone 1, then select "air fry" mode and set the temperature to 360 degrees F for 10 minutes. Press "match" to match zone 2 settings to zone 1. Press "start/stop" to begin.

Nutrition Info:
- (Per serving) Calories 393 | Fat 7.4g |Sodium 351mg | Carbs 43.4g | Fiber 2.1g | Sugar 1.8g | Protein 35.7g

Roasted Salmon And Parmesan Asparagus

Servings: 4 | Cooking Time: 27 Minutes

Ingredients:
- 2 tablespoons Montreal steak seasoning
- 3 tablespoons brown sugar
- 3 uncooked salmon fillets (6 ounces each)
- 2 tablespoons canola oil, divided
- 1-pound asparagus, ends trimmed
- Kosher salt, as desired
- Ground black pepper, as desired
- ¼ cup shredded parmesan cheese, divided

Directions:
1. Combine the steak spice and brown sugar in a small bowl.
2. Brush 1 tablespoon of oil over the salmon fillets, then thoroughly coat with the sugar mixture.
3. Toss the asparagus with the remaining 1 tablespoon of oil, salt, and pepper in a mixing bowl.
4. Place a crisper plate in both drawers. Put the fillets skin-side down in the zone 1 drawer, then place the drawer in the unit. Insert the zone 2 drawer into the device after placing the asparagus in it.
5. Select zone 1, then ROAST, then set the temperature to 390 degrees F/ 200 degrees C with a 17-minute timer. To match the zone 2 settings to zone 1, choose MATCH. To begin cooking, press the START/STOP button.
6. When the zone 2 timer reaches 7 minutes, press START/STOP. Remove the zone 2 drawer from the unit. Flip the asparagus with silicone-tipped tongs. Re-insert the drawer into the unit. Continue cooking by pressing START/STOP.
7. When the zone 2 timer has reached 14 minutes, press START/STOP. Remove the zone 2 drawer from the unit. Sprinkle half the parmesan cheese over the asparagus, and mix lightly. Re-insert the drawer into the unit. Continue cooking by pressing START/STOP.
8. Transfer the fillets and asparagus to a serving plate once they've finished cooking. Serve with the remaining parmesan cheese on top of the asparagus.

Nutrition Info:
- (Per serving) Calories 293 | Fat 15.8g | Sodium 203mg | Carbs 11.1g | Fiber 2.4g | Sugar 8.7g | Protein 29g

Crispy Catfish

Servings: 4 | Cooking Time: 17 Minutes.

Ingredients:
- 4 catfish fillets
- ¼ cup Louisiana Fish fry
- 1 tablespoon olive oil
- 1 tablespoon parsley, chopped
- 1 lemon, sliced
- Fresh herbs, to garnish

Directions:
1. Mix fish fry with olive oil, and parsley then liberally rub over the catfish.
2. Place two fillets in each of the crisper plate.
3. Return the crisper plates to the Ninja Foodi Dual Zone Air Fryer.
4. Choose the Air Fry mode for Zone 1 and set the temperature to 390 degrees F and the time to 17 minutes.
5. Select the "MATCH" button to copy the settings for Zone 2.
6. Initiate cooking by pressing the START/STOP button.
7. Garnish with lemon slices and herbs.
8. Serve warm.

Nutrition Info:
- (Per serving) Calories 275 | Fat 1.4g | Sodium 582mg | Carbs 31.5g | Fiber 1.1g | Sugar 0.1g | Protein 29.8g

Broiled Teriyaki Salmon With Eggplant In Stir-fry Sauce

Servings: 4 | Cooking Time: 25 Minutes

Ingredients:

- FOR THE TERIYAKI SALMON
- 4 salmon fillets (6 ounces each)
- ½ cup teriyaki sauce
- 3 scallions, sliced
- FOR THE EGGPLANT
- ¼ cup reduced-sodium soy sauce
- ¼ cup packed light brown sugar
- 1 tablespoon minced fresh ginger
- 1 tablespoon minced garlic
- 2 teaspoons sesame oil
- ¼ teaspoon red pepper flakes
- 1 eggplant, peeled and cut into bite-size cubes
- Nonstick cooking spray

Directions:

1. To prep the teriyaki salmon: Brush the top of each salmon fillet with the teriyaki sauce.
2. To prep the eggplant: In a small bowl, whisk together the soy sauce, brown sugar, ginger, garlic, sesame oil, and red pepper flakes. Set the stir-fry sauce aside.
3. Spritz the eggplant cubes with cooking spray.
4. To cook the salmon and eggplant: Install a crisper plate in each of the two baskets. Place the salmon in a single layer in the Zone 1 basket and insert the basket in the unit. Place the eggplant in the Zone 2 basket and insert the basket in the unit.
5. Select Zone 1, select AIR BROIL, set the temperature to 450°F, and set the time to 8 minutes.
6. Select Zone 2, select AIR FRY, set the temperature to 390°F, and set the time to 25 minutes. Select SMART FINISH.
7. Press START/PAUSE to begin cooking.
8. When the Zone 2 timer reads 5 minutes, press START/PAUSE. Remove the basket and pour the stir-fry sauce evenly over the eggplant. Shake or stir to coat the eggplant cubes in the sauce. Reinsert the basket and press START/PAUSE to resume cooking.
9. When cooking is complete, the salmon should be cooked to your liking and the eggplant tender and slightly caramelized. Serve hot.

Nutrition Info:

- (Per serving) Calories: 499; Total fat: 22g; Saturated fat: 2g; Carbohydrates: 36g; Fiber: 3.5g; Protein: 42g; Sodium: 1,024mg

Furikake Salmon

Servings: 4 | Cooking Time: 10 Minutes

Ingredients:

- ½ cup mayonnaise
- 1 tablespoon shoyu
- 455g salmon fillet
- Salt and black pepper to taste
- 2 tablespoons furikake

Directions:

1. Mix shoyu with mayonnaise in a small bowl.
2. Rub the salmon with black pepper and salt.
3. Place the salmon pieces in the air fryer baskets.
4. Top them with the mayo mixture.
5. Return the air fryer basket 1 to Zone 1, and basket 2 to Zone 2 of the Ninja Foodi 2-Basket Air Fryer.
6. Choose the "Air Fry" mode for Zone 1 at 400 degrees F and 10 minutes of cooking time.
7. Select the "MATCH COOK" option to copy the settings for Zone 2.
8. Initiate cooking by pressing the START/PAUSE BUTTON.
9. Serve warm.

Nutrition Info:

- (Per serving) Calories 297 | Fat 1g | Sodium 291mg | Carbs 35g | Fiber 1g | Sugar 9g | Protein 29g

Fish Sandwich

Servings: 4 | Cooking Time: 22 Minutes.

Ingredients:
- 4 small cod fillets, skinless
- Salt and black pepper, to taste
- 2 tablespoons flour
- ¼ cup dried breadcrumbs
- Spray oil
- 9 ounces of frozen peas
- 1 tablespoon creme fraiche
- 12 capers
- 1 squeeze of lemon juice
- 4 bread rolls, cut in halve

Directions:
1. First, coat the cod fillets with flour, salt, and black pepper.
2. Then coat the fish with breadcrumbs.
3. Divide the coated codfish in the two crisper plates and spray them with cooking spray.
4. Return the crisper plate to the Ninja Foodi Dual Zone Air Fryer.
5. Choose the Air Fry mode for Zone 1 and set the temperature to 390 degrees F and the time to 17 minutes.
6. Select the "MATCH" button to copy the settings for Zone 2.
7. Initiate cooking by pressing the START/STOP button.
8. Meanwhile, boil peas in hot water for 5 minutes until soft.
9. Then drain the peas and transfer them to the blender.
10. Add capers, lemon juice, and crème fraiche to the blender.
11. Blend until it makes a smooth mixture.
12. Spread the peas crème mixture on top of 2 lower halves of the bread roll, and place the fish fillets on it.
13. Place the remaining bread slices on top.
14. Serve fresh.

Nutrition Info:
- (Per serving) Calories 348 | Fat 30g | Sodium 660mg | Carbs 5g | Fiber 0g | Sugar 0g | Protein 14g

Fried Tilapia

Servings: 4 | Cooking Time: 20 Minutes

Ingredients:
- 4 fresh tilapia fillets, approximately 6 ounces each
- 2 teaspoons olive oil
- 2 teaspoons chopped fresh chives
- 2 teaspoons chopped fresh parsley
- 1 teaspoon minced garlic
- Freshly ground pepper, to taste
- Salt to taste

Directions:
1. Pat the tilapia fillets dry with a paper towel.
2. Stir together the olive oil, chives, parsley, garlic, salt, and pepper in a small bowl.
3. Brush the mixture over the top of the tilapia fillets.
4. Place a crisper plate in each drawer. Add the fillets in a single layer to each drawer. Insert the drawers into the unit.
5. Select zone 1, then AIR FRY, then set the temperature to 360 degrees F/ 180 degrees C with a 20-minute timer. To match zone 2 settings to zone 1, choose MATCH. To begin, select START/STOP.
6. Remove the tilapia fillets from the drawers after the timer has finished.

Nutrition Info:
- (Per serving) Calories 140 | Fat 5.7g | Sodium 125mg | Carbs 1.5g | Fiber 0.4g | Sugar 0g | Protein 21.7g

Tilapia With Mojo And Crispy Plantains

Servings: 4 | Cooking Time: 30 Minutes

Ingredients:
- FOR THE TILAPIA
- 4 tilapia fillets (6 ounces each)
- 2 tablespoons all-purpose flour
- Nonstick cooking spray
- ¼ cup freshly squeezed orange juice
- 3 tablespoons fresh lime juice
- 2 tablespoons olive oil
- 1 tablespoon minced garlic
- ½ teaspoon ground cumin
- ¼ teaspoon kosher salt
- FOR THE PLANTAINS
- 1 large green plantain
- 2 cups cold water
- 2 teaspoons kosher salt
- Nonstick cooking spray

Directions:
1. To prep the tilapia: Dust both sides of the tilapia fillets with the flour, then spritz with cooking spray.
2. In a small bowl, whisk together the orange juice, lime juice, oil, garlic, cumin, and salt. Set the mojo sauce aside.
3. To prep the plantains: Cut the ends from the plantain, then remove and discard the peel. Slice the plantain into 1-inch rounds.
4. In a large bowl, combine the water, salt, and plantains. Let soak for 15 minutes.
5. Drain the plantains and pat them dry with paper towels. Spray with cooking spray.
6. To cook the tilapia and plantains: Install a crisper plate in each of the two baskets. Place the tilapia in a single layer in the Zone 1 basket (work in batches if needed) and insert the basket in the unit. Place the plantains in the Zone 2 basket and insert the basket in the unit.
7. Select Zone 1, select AIR FRY, set the temperature to 390°F, and set the timer to 10 minutes.
8. Select Zone 2, select AIR FRY, set the temperature to 390°F, and set the timer to 30 minutes. Select SMART FINISH.
9. Press START/PAUSE to begin cooking.
10. When the Zone 2 timer reads 10 minutes, press START/PAUSE. Remove the basket and use silicone-tipped tongs to transfer the plantains, which should be tender, to a cutting board. Use the bottom of a heavy glass to smash each plantain flat. Spray both sides with cooking spray and place them back in the basket. Reinsert the basket and press START/PAUSE to resume cooking.
11. When the Zone 1 timer reads 5 minutes, press START/PAUSE. Remove the basket. Spoon half of the mojo sauce over the tilapia. Reinsert the basket and press START/PAUSE to resume cooking.
12. When cooking is complete, the fish should be cooked through and the plantains crispy. Serve the tilapia and plantains with the remaining mojo sauce for dipping.

Nutrition Info:
- (Per serving) Calories: 380; Total fat: 21g; Saturated fat: 2g; Carbohydrates: 20g; Fiber: 1g; Protein: 35g; Sodium: 217mg

Salmon Nuggets

Servings: 4 | Cooking Time: 15 Minutes.

Ingredients:
- ⅓ cup maple syrup
- ¼ teaspoon dried chipotle pepper
- 1 pinch sea salt
- 1 ½ cups croutons
- 1 large egg
- 1 (1 pound) skinless salmon fillet, cut into 1 ½-inch chunk
- cooking spray

Directions:
1. Mix chipotle powder, maple syrup, and salt in a saucepan and cook on a simmer for 5 minutes.
2. Crush the croutons in a food processor and transfer to a bowl.
3. Beat egg in another shallow bowl.
4. Season the salmon chunks with sea salt.
5. Dip the salmon in the egg, then coat with breadcrumbs.
6. Divide the coated salmon chunks in the two crisper plates.
7. Return the crisper plate to the Ninja Foodi Dual Zone Air Fryer.
8. Select the Air Fry mode for Zone 1 and set the temperature to 390 degrees F and the time to 10 minutes.
9. Press the "MATCH" button to copy the settings for Zone 2.
10. Initiate cooking by pressing the START/STOP button.
11. Flip the chunks once cooked halfway through, then resume cooking.
12. Pour the maple syrup on top and serve warm.

Nutrition Info:
- (Per serving) Calories 275 | Fat 1.4g | Sodium 582mg | Carbs 31.5g | Fiber 1.1g | Sugar 0.1g | Protein 29.8g

Bacon-wrapped Shrimp

Servings: 8 | Cooking Time: 10 Minutes

Ingredients:
- 24 jumbo raw shrimp, deveined with tail on, fresh or thawed from frozen
- 8 slices bacon, cut into thirds
- 1 tablespoon olive oil
- 1 teaspoon paprika
- 1–2 cloves minced garlic
- 1 tablespoon finely chopped fresh parsley

Directions:
1. Combine the olive oil, paprika, garlic, and parsley in a small bowl.
2. If necessary, peel the raw shrimp, leaving the tails on.
3. Add the shrimp to the oil mixture. Toss to coat well.
4. Wrap a piece of bacon around the middle of each shrimp and place seam-side down on a small baking dish.
5. Refrigerate for 30 minutes before cooking.
6. Place a crisper plate in each drawer. Put the shrimp in a single layer in each drawer. Insert the drawers into the unit.
7. Select zone 1, then AIR FRY, then set the temperature to 360 degrees F/ 180 degrees C with a 10-minute timer. To match zone 2 settings to zone 1, choose MATCH. To begin, select START/STOP.
8. Remove the shrimp from the drawers when the cooking time is over.

Nutrition Info:
- (Per serving) Calories 479 | Fat 15.7g | Sodium 949mg | Carbs 0.6g | Fiber 0.1g | Sugar 0g | Protein 76.1g

Shrimp Po'boys With Sweet Potato Fries

Servings: 4 | Cooking Time: 30 Minutes

Ingredients:

- FOR THE SHRIMP PO'BOYS
- ½ cup buttermilk
- 1 tablespoon Louisiana-style hot sauce
- ¾ cup all-purpose flour
- ½ cup cornmeal
- ½ teaspoon kosher salt
- ½ teaspoon paprika
- ½ teaspoon garlic powder
- ½ teaspoon freshly ground black pepper
- 1 pound peeled medium shrimp, thawed if frozen
- Nonstock cooking spray
- ½ cup store-bought rémoulade sauce
- 4 French bread rolls, halved lengthwise
- ½ cup shredded lettuce
- 1 tomato, sliced
- FOR THE SWEET POTATO FRIES
- 2 medium sweet potatoes
- 2 teaspoons vegetable oil
- ¼ teaspoon garlic powder
- ¼ teaspoon paprika
- ¼ teaspoon kosher salt

Directions:

1. To prep the shrimp: In a medium bowl, combine the buttermilk and hot sauce. In a shallow bowl, combine the flour, cornmeal, salt, paprika, garlic powder, and black pepper.
2. Add the shrimp to the buttermilk and stir to coat. Remove the shrimp, letting the excess buttermilk drip off, then add to the cornmeal mixture to coat.
3. Spritz the breaded shrimp with cooking spray, then let sit for 10 minutes.
4. To prep the sweet potatoes: Peel the sweet potatoes and cut them lengthwise into ¼-inch-thick sticks (like shoestring fries).
5. In a large bowl, combine the sweet potatoes, oil, garlic powder, paprika, and salt. Toss to coat.
6. To cook the shrimp and fries: Install a crisper plate in each of the two baskets. Place the shrimp in the Zone 1 basket and insert the basket in the unit. Place the sweet potatoes in a single layer in the Zone 2 basket and insert the basket in the unit.
7. Select Zone 1, select AIR FRY, set the temperature to 390°F, and set the timer to 13 minutes.
8. Select Zone 2, select AIR FRY, set the temperature to 400°F, and set the timer to 30 minutes. Select SMART FINISH.
9. Press START/PAUSE to begin cooking.
10. When cooking is complete, the shrimp should be golden and cooked through and the sweet potato fries crisp.
11. Spread the rémoulade on the cut sides of the rolls. Divide the lettuce and tomato among the rolls, then top with the fried shrimp. Serve with the sweet potato fries on the side.

Nutrition Info:

- (Per serving) Calories: 669; Total fat: 22g; Saturated fat: 2g; Carbohydrates: 86g; Fiber: 3.5g; Protein: 33g; Sodium: 1,020mg

Glazed Scallops

Servings: 6 | Cooking Time: 13 Minutes.

Ingredients:

- 12 scallops
- 3 tablespoons olive oil
- Black pepper and salt to taste

Directions:

1. Rub the scallops with olive oil, black pepper, and salt.
2. Divide the scallops in the two crisper plates.
3. Return the crisper plate to the Ninja Foodi Dual Zone Air Fryer.
4. Choose the Air Fry mode for Zone 1 and set the temperature to 390 degrees F and the time to 13 minutes.
5. Select the "MATCH" button to copy the settings for Zone 2.
6. Initiate cooking by pressing the START/STOP button.
7. Flip the scallops once cooked halfway through, and resume cooking.
8. Serve warm.

Nutrition Info:

- (Per serving) Calories 308 | Fat 24g | Sodium 715mg | Carbs 0.8g | Fiber 0.1g | Sugar 0.1g | Protein 21.9g

Vegetables And Sides Recipes

Fried Olives 55

Kale And Spinach Chips.. 55

Mushroom Roll-ups 56

Lime Glazed Tofu 56

Bacon Wrapped Corn Cob 57

Zucchini Cakes.. 57

Bacon Potato Patties... 58

Green Tomato Stacks.. 58

Stuffed Tomatoes 59

Green Salad With Crispy Fried Goat Cheese And Baked Croutons.. 59

Lemon Herb Cauliflower.. 60

Fried Avocado Tacos 60

Fresh Mix Veggies In Air Fryer 61

Chickpea Fritters 61

Brussels Sprouts 62

Quinoa Patties... 62

Vegetables And Sides Recipes

Fried Olives

Servings: 6 | Cooking Time: 9 Minutes.

Ingredients:
- 2 cups blue cheese stuffed olives, drained
- ½ cup all-purpose flour
- 1 cup panko breadcrumbs
- ½ teaspoon garlic powder
- 1 pinch oregano
- 2 eggs

Directions:
1. Mix flour with oregano and garlic powder in a bowl and beat two eggs in another bowl.
2. Spread panko breadcrumbs in a bowl.
3. Coat all the olives with the flour mixture, dip in the eggs and then coat with the panko breadcrumbs.
4. As you coat the olives, place them in the two crisper plates in a single layer, then spray them with cooking oil.
5. Return the crisper plates to the Ninja Foodi Dual Zone Air Fryer.
6. Choose the Air Fry mode for Zone 1 and set the temperature to 375 degrees F and the time to 9 minutes.
7. Select the "MATCH" button to copy the settings for Zone 2.
8. Initiate cooking by pressing the START/STOP button.
9. Flip the olives once cooked halfway through, then resume cooking.
10. Serve.

Nutrition Info:
- (Per serving) Calories 166 | Fat 3.2g | Sodium 437mg | Carbs 28.8g | Fiber 1.8g | Sugar 2.7g | Protein 5.8g

Kale And Spinach Chips

Servings: 2 | Cooking Time: 6

Ingredients:
- 2 cups spinach, torn in pieces and stem removed
- 2 cups kale, torn in pieces, stems removed
- 1 tablespoon of olive oil
- Sea salt, to taste
- 1/3 cup Parmesan cheese

Directions:
1. Take a bowl and add spinach to it.
2. Take another bowl and add kale to it.
3. Now, season both of them with olive oil, and sea salt.
4. Add kale to zone 1 basket and spinach to zone 2 basket.
5. Select the zone 1 air fry mode at 350 degrees F for 6 minutes.
6. Set zone 2 to AIR FRY mode at 350 for 5 minutes.
7. Once done, take out the crispy chips and sprinkle Parmesan cheese on top.
8. Serve and Enjoy.

Nutrition Info:
- (Per serving) Calories 166 | Fat 11.1g | Sodium 355mg | Carbs 8.1g | Fiber 1.7g | Sugar 0.1g | Protein 8.2g

Mushroom Roll-ups

Servings: 10 | Cooking Time: 11 Minutes.

Ingredients:
- 2 tablespoons olive oil
- 227g portobello mushrooms, chopped
- 1 teaspoon dried oregano
- 1 teaspoon dried thyme
- ½ teaspoon crushed red pepper flakes
- ¼ teaspoon salt
- 1 package (227g) cream cheese, softened
- 113g whole-milk ricotta cheese
- 10 (8 inches) flour tortillas
- Cooking spray
- Chutney

Directions:
1. Sauté mushrooms with oil, thyme, salt, pepper flakes, and oregano in a skillet for 4 minutes.
2. Mix cheeses and add sauteed mushrooms the mix well.
3. Divide the mushroom mixture over the tortillas.
4. Roll the tortillas and secure with a toothpick.
5. Place the rolls in the air fryer basket.
6. Return the air fryer basket 1 to Zone 1, and basket 2 to Zone 2 of the Ninja Foodi 2-Basket Air Fryer.
7. Choose the "Air Fry" mode for Zone 1 and set the temperature to 400 degrees F and 11 minutes of cooking time.
8. Select the "MATCH COOK" option to copy the settings for Zone 2.
9. Initiate cooking by pressing the START/PAUSE BUTTON.
10. Flip the rolls once cooked halfway through.
11. Serve warm.

Nutrition Info:
- (Per serving) Calories 288 | Fat 6.9g | Sodium 761mg | Carbs 46g | Fiber 4g | Sugar 12g | Protein 9.6g

Lime Glazed Tofu

Servings: 6 | Cooking Time: 14 Minutes.

Ingredients:
- ⅔ cup coconut aminos
- 2 (14-oz) packages extra-firm, water-packed tofu, drained
- 6 tablespoons toasted sesame oil
- ⅔ cup lime juice

Directions:
1. Pat dry the tofu bars and slice into half-inch cubes.
2. Toss all the remaining ingredients in a small bowl.
3. Marinate for 4 hours in the refrigerator. Drain off the excess water.
4. Divide the tofu cubes in the two crisper plates.
5. Return the crisper plates to the Ninja Foodi Dual Zone Air Fryer.
6. Choose the Air Fry mode for Zone 1 and set the temperature to 400 degrees F and the time to 14 minutes.
7. Select the "MATCH" button to copy the settings for Zone 2.
8. Initiate cooking by pressing the START/STOP button.
9. Toss the tofu once cooked halfway through, then resume cooking.
10. Serve warm.

Nutrition Info:
- (Per serving) Calories 284 | Fat 7.9g | Sodium 704mg | Carbs 38.1g | Fiber 1.9g | Sugar 1.9g | Protein 14.8g

Bacon Wrapped Corn Cob

Servings: 4 | Cooking Time: 10 Minutes

Ingredients:
- 4 trimmed corns on the cob
- 8 bacon slices

Directions:
1. Wrap the corn cobs with two bacon slices.
2. Place the wrapped cobs into the Ninja Foodi 2 Baskets Air Fryer baskets.
3. Return the air fryer basket 1 to Zone 1, and basket 2 to Zone 2 of the Ninja Foodi 2-Basket Air Fryer.
4. Choose the "Air Fry" mode for Zone 1 and set the temperature to 355 degrees F and 10 minutes of cooking time.
5. Select the "MATCH COOK" option to copy the settings for Zone 2.
6. Initiate cooking by pressing the START/PAUSE BUTTON.
7. Flip the corn cob once cooked halfway through.
8. Serve warm.

Nutrition Info:
- (Per serving) Calories 350 | Fat 2.6g | Sodium 358mg | Carbs 64.6g | Fiber 14.4g | Sugar 3.3g | Protein 19.9g

Zucchini Cakes

Servings: 6 | Cooking Time: 32 Minutes.

Ingredients:
- 2 medium zucchinis, grated
- 1 cup corn kernel
- 1 medium potato cooked
- 2 tablespoons chickpea flour
- 2 garlic minced
- 2 teaspoons olive oil
- Salt and black pepper
- For Serving:
- Yogurt tahini sauce

Directions:
1. Mix grated zucchini with a pinch of salt in a colander and leave them for 15 minutes.
2. Squeeze out their excess water.
3. Mash the cooked potato in a large-sized bowl with a fork.
4. Add zucchini, corn, garlic, chickpea flour, salt, and black pepper to the bowl.
5. Mix these fritters' ingredients together and make 2 tablespoons-sized balls out of this mixture and flatten them lightly.
6. Divide the fritters in the two crisper plates in a single layer and spray them with cooking.
7. Return the crisper plates to the Ninja Foodi Dual Zone Air Fryer.
8. Choose the Air Fry mode for Zone 1 and set the temperature to 390 degrees F and the time to 17 minutes.
9. Select the "MATCH" button to copy the settings for Zone 2.
10. Initiate cooking by pressing the START/STOP button.
11. Flip the fritters once cooked halfway through, then resume cooking.
12. Serve.

Nutrition Info:
- (Per serving) Calories 270 | Fat 14.6g | Sodium 394mg | Carbs 31.3g | Fiber 7.5g | Sugar 9.7g | Protein 6.4g

Bacon Potato Patties

Servings: 2 | Cooking Time: 15 Minutes

Ingredients:
- 1 egg
- 600g mashed potatoes
- 119g breadcrumbs
- 2 bacon slices, cooked & chopped
- 235g cheddar cheese, shredded
- 15g flour
- Pepper
- Salt

Directions:
1. In a bowl, mix mashed potatoes with remaining ingredients until well combined.
2. Make patties from potato mixture and place on a plate.
3. Place plate in the refrigerator for 10 minutes
4. Insert a crisper plate in the Ninja Foodi air fryer baskets.
5. Place the prepared patties in both baskets.
6. Select zone 1 then select "air fry" mode and set the temperature to 390 degrees F for 15 minutes. Press "match" to match zone 2 settings to zone 1. Press "start/stop" to begin. Turn halfway through.

Nutrition Info:
- (Per serving) Calories 702 | Fat 26.8g | Sodium 1405mg | Carbs 84.8g | Fiber 2.7g | Sugar 3.8g | Protein 30.5g

Green Tomato Stacks

Servings: 6 | Cooking Time: 12 Minutes

Ingredients:
- ¼ cup mayonnaise
- ¼ teaspoon lime zest, grated
- 2 tablespoons lime juice
- 1 teaspoon minced fresh thyme
- ½ teaspoon black pepper
- ¼ cup all-purpose flour
- 2 large egg whites, beaten
- ¾ cup cornmeal
- ¼ teaspoon salt
- 2 medium green tomatoes
- 2 medium re tomatoes
- Cooking spray
- 8 slices Canadian bacon, warmed

Directions:
1. Mix mayonnaise with ¼ teaspoon black pepper, thyme, lime juice and zest in a bowl.
2. Spread flour in one bowl, beat egg whites in another bowl and mix cornmeal with ¼ teaspoon black pepper and salt in a third bowl.
3. Cut the tomatoes into 4 slices and coat each with the flour then dip in the egg whites.
4. Coat the tomatoes slices with the cornmeal mixture.
5. Place the slices in the air fryer baskets.
6. Return the air fryer basket 1 to Zone 1, and basket 2 to Zone 2 of the Ninja Foodi 2-Basket Air Fryer.
7. Choose the "Air Fry" mode for Zone 1 at 390 degrees F and 12 minutes of cooking time.
8. Select the "MATCH COOK" option to copy the settings for Zone 2.
9. Initiate cooking by pressing the START/PAUSE BUTTON.
10. Flip the tomatoes once cooked halfway through.
11. Place the green tomato slices on the working surface.
12. Top them with bacon, and red tomato slice.
13. Serve.

Nutrition Info:
- (Per serving) Calories 113 | Fat 3g | Sodium 152mg | Carbs 20g | Fiber 3g | Sugar 1.1g | Protein 3.5g

Stuffed Tomatoes

Servings:2 | Cooking Time:8

Ingredients:
- 2 cups brown rice, cooked
- 1 cup of tofu, grilled and chopped
- 4 large red tomatoes
- 4 tablespoons basil, chopped
- 1/4 tablespoon olive oil
- Salt and black pepper, to taste
- 2 tablespoons of lemon juice
- 1 teaspoon of red chili powder
- ½ cup Parmesan cheese

Directions:
1. Take a large bowl and mix rice, tofu, basil, olive oil, salt, black pepper, lemon juice, and chili powder.
2. Take four large tomatoes and center core them.
3. Fill the cavity with the rice mixture.
4. Top it off with the cheese sprinkle.
5. Divide the tomatoes into two air fryer baskets.
6. turn on zone one basket and cook tomatoes at AIRFRY mode, for 8 minutes at 400 degrees F.
7. Select the MATCH button for zone two baskets, which cooks food by copying the setting across both zones.
8. Serve and enjoy.

Nutrition Info:
- (Per serving) Calories 1034| Fat 24.2g| Sodium 527mg | Carbs165 g | Fiber12.1 g | Sugar 1.2g | Protein 43.9g

Green Salad With Crispy Fried Goat Cheese And Baked Croutons

Servings:4 | Cooking Time: 10 Minutes

Ingredients:
- FOR THE GOAT CHEESE
- 1 (4-ounce) log soft goat cheese
- ½ cup panko bread crumbs
- 2 tablespoons vegetable oil
- FOR THE CROUTONS
- 2 slices Italian-style sandwich bread
- 2 tablespoons vegetable oil
- 1 tablespoon poultry seasoning
- ½ teaspoon kosher salt
- ¼ teaspoon freshly ground black pepper
- FOR THE SALAD
- 8 cups green leaf lettuce leaves
- ½ cup store-bought balsamic vinaigrette

Directions:
1. To prep the goat cheese: Cut the goat cheese into 8 round slices.
2. Spread the panko on a plate. Gently press the cheese into the panko to coat on both sides. Drizzle with the oil.
3. To prep the croutons: Cut the bread into cubes and place them in a large bowl. Add the oil, poultry seasoning, salt, and black pepper. Mix well to coat the bread cubes evenly.
4. To cook the goat cheese and croutons: Install a crisper plate in each of the two baskets. Place the goat cheese in the Zone 1 basket and insert the basket in the unit. Place the croutons in the Zone 2 basket and insert the basket in the unit.
5. Select Zone 1, select AIR FRY, set the temperature to 400°F, and set the timer to 6 minutes.
6. Select Zone 2, select BAKE, set the temperature to 390°F, and set the timer to 10 minutes. Select SMART FINISH.
7. Press START/PAUSE to begin cooking.
8. When cooking is complete, the goat cheese will be golden brown and the croutons crisp.
9. Remove the Zone 1 basket. Let the goat cheese cool in the basket for 5 minutes; it will firm up as it cools.
10. To assemble the salad: In a large bowl, combine the lettuce, vinaigrette, and croutons. Toss well. Divide the salad among four plates. Top each plate with 2 pieces of goat cheese.

Nutrition Info:
- (Per serving) Calories: 578; Total fat: 40g; Saturated fat: 14g; Carbohydrates: 39g; Fiber: 3.5g; Protein: 24g; Sodium: 815mg

Lemon Herb Cauliflower

Servings: 4 | Cooking Time: 10 Minutes

Ingredients:
- 384g cauliflower florets
- 1 tsp lemon zest, grated
- 1 tbsp thyme, minced
- 60ml olive oil
- 1 tbsp rosemary, minced
- ¼ tsp red pepper flakes, crushed
- 30ml lemon juice
- 25g parsley, minced
- ½ tsp salt

Directions:
1. In a bowl, toss cauliflower florets with the remaining ingredients until well coated.
2. Insert a crisper plate in the Ninja Foodi air fryer baskets.
3. Add cauliflower florets into both baskets.
4. Select zone 1, then select "air fry" mode and set the temperature to 360 degrees F for 10 minutes. Press "match" and "start/stop" to begin.

Nutrition Info:
- (Per serving) Calories 166 | Fat 14.4g | Sodium 340mg | Carbs 9.5g | Fiber 4.6g | Sugar 3.8g | Protein 3.3g

Fried Avocado Tacos

Servings: 4 | Cooking Time: 10 Minutes

Ingredients:
- For the sauce:
- 2 cups shredded fresh kale or coleslaw mix
- ¼ cup minced fresh cilantro
- ¼ cup plain Greek yogurt
- 2 tablespoons lime juice
- 1 teaspoon honey
- ¼ teaspoon salt
- ¼ teaspoon ground chipotle pepper
- ¼ teaspoon pepper
- For the tacos:
- 1 large egg, beaten
- ¼ cup cornmeal
- ½ teaspoon salt
- ½ teaspoon garlic powder
- ½ teaspoon ground chipotle pepper
- 2 medium avocados, peeled and sliced
- Cooking spray
- 8 flour tortillas or corn tortillas (6 inches), heated up
- 1 medium tomato, chopped
- Crumbled queso fresco (optional)

Directions:
1. Combine the first 8 ingredients in a bowl. Cover and refrigerate until serving.
2. Place the egg in a shallow bowl. In another shallow bowl, mix the cornmeal, salt, garlic powder, and chipotle pepper.
3. Dip the avocado slices in the egg, then into the cornmeal mixture, gently patting to help adhere.
4. Place a crisper plate in both drawers. Put the avocado slices in the drawers in a single layer. Insert the drawers into the unit.
5. Select zone 1, then AIR FRY, then set the temperature to 360 degrees F/ 180 degrees C with a 6-minute timer. To match zone 2 settings to zone 1, choose MATCH. To begin, select START/STOP.
6. Put the avocado slices, prepared sauce, tomato, and queso fresco in the tortillas and serve.

Nutrition Info:
- (Per serving) Calories 407 | Fat 21g | Sodium 738mg | Carbs 48g | Fiber 4g | Sugar 9g | Protein 9g

Fresh Mix Veggies In Air Fryer

Servings:4 | Cooking Time:12

Ingredients:
- 1 cup cauliflower florets
- 1 cup of carrots, peeled chopped
- 1 cup broccoli florets
- 2 tablespoons of avocado oil
- Salt, to taste
- ½ teaspoon of chili powder
- ½ teaspoon of garlic powder
- ½ teaspoon of herbs de Provence
- 1 cup parmesan cheese

Directions:
1. Take a bowl, and add all the veggies to it.
2. Toss and then season the veggies with salt, chili powder, garlic powder, and herbs de Provence.
3. Toss it all well and then drizzle avocado oil.
4. Make sure the ingredients are coated well.
5. Now distribute the veggies among both baskets of the air fryer.
6. Turn on the start button and set it to AIR FRY mode at 390 degrees for 10-12 minutes.
7. For the zone 2 basket setting, press the MATCH button.
8. After 8 minutes of cooking, select the pause button and then take out the baskets and sprinkle Parmesan cheese on top of the veggies.
9. Then let the cooking cycle complete for the next 3-4 minutes.
10. Once done, serve.

Nutrition Info:
- (Per serving) Calories161 | Fat 9.3g| Sodium434 mg | Carbs 7.7g | Fiber 2.4g | Sugar 2.5g | Protein 13.9

Chickpea Fritters

Servings: 6 | Cooking Time: 6 Minutes

Ingredients:
- 237ml plain yogurt
- 2 tablespoons sugar
- 1 tablespoon honey
- ½ teaspoon salt
- ½ teaspoon black pepper
- ½ teaspoon crushed red pepper flakes
- 1 can (28g) chickpeas, drained
- 1 teaspoon ground cumin
- ½ teaspoon salt
- ½ teaspoon garlic powder
- ½ teaspoon ground ginger
- 1 large egg
- ½ teaspoon baking soda
- ½ cup fresh coriander, chopped
- 2 green onions, sliced

Directions:
1. Mash chickpeas with rest of the ingredients in a food processor.
2. Layer the two air fryer baskets with a parchment paper.
3. Drop the batter in the baskets spoon by spoon.
4. Return the air fryer basket 1 to Zone 1, and basket 2 to Zone 2 of the Ninja Foodi 2-Basket Air Fryer.
5. Choose the "Air Fry" mode for Zone 1 at 400 degrees F and 6 minutes of cooking time.
6. Select the "MATCH COOK" option to copy the settings for Zone 2.
7. Initiate cooking by pressing the START/PAUSE BUTTON.
8. Flip the fritters once cooked halfway through.
9. Serve warm.

Nutrition Info:
- (Per serving) Calories 284 | Fat 7.9g |Sodium 704mg | Carbs 38.1g | Fiber 1.9g | Sugar 1.9g | Protein 14.8g

Brussels Sprouts

Servings: 2 | Cooking Time: 20

Ingredients:
- 2 pounds Brussels sprouts
- 2 tablespoons avocado oil
- Salt and pepper, to taste
- 1 cup pine nuts, roasted

Directions:
1. Trim the bottom of Brussels sprouts.
2. Take a bowl and combine the avocado oil, salt, and black pepper.
3. Toss the Brussels sprouts well.
4. Divide it in both air fryer baskets.
5. For the zone 1 basket use AIR fry mode for 20 minutes at 390 degrees F.
6. Select the MATCH button for the zone 2 basket.
7. Once the Brussels sprouts get crisp and tender, take out and serve.

Nutrition Info:
- (Per serving) Calories 672| Fat 50g| Sodium 115mg | Carbs 51g | Fiber 20.2g | Sugar 12.3g | Protein 25g

Quinoa Patties

Servings: 4 | Cooking Time: 32 Minutes.

Ingredients:
- 1 cup quinoa red
- 1½ cups water
- 1 teaspoon salt
- black pepper, ground
- 1½ cups rolled oats
- 3 eggs beaten
- ¼ cup minced white onion
- ½ cup crumbled feta cheese
- ¼ cup chopped fresh chives
- Salt and black pepper, to taste
- Vegetable or canola oil
- 4 hamburger buns
- 4 arugulas
- 4 slices tomato sliced
- Cucumber yogurt dill sauce
- 1 cup cucumber, diced
- 1 cup Greek yogurt
- 2 teaspoons lemon juice
- ¼ teaspoon salt
- Black pepper, ground
- 1 tablespoon chopped fresh dill
- 1 tablespoon olive oil

Directions:
1. Add quinoa to a saucepan filled with cold water, salt, and black pepper, and place it over medium-high heat.
2. Cook the quinoa to a boil, then reduce the heat, cover, and cook for 20 minutes on a simmer.
3. Fluff and mix the cooked quinoa with a fork and remove it from the heat.
4. Spread the quinoa in a baking stay.
5. Mix eggs, oats, onion, herbs, cheese, salt, and black pepper.
6. Stir in quinoa, then mix well. Make 4 patties out of this quinoa cheese mixture.
7. Divide the patties in the two crisper plates and spray them with cooking oil.
8. Return the crisper plates to the Ninja Foodi Dual Zone Air Fryer.
9. Choose the Air Fry mode for Zone 1 and set the temperature to 390 degrees F and the time to 13 minutes.
10. Select the "MATCH" button to copy the settings for Zone 2.
11. Initiate cooking by pressing the START/STOP button.
12. Flip the patties once cooked halfway through, and resume cooking.
13. Meanwhile, prepare the cucumber yogurt dill sauce by mixing all of its ingredients in a mixing bowl.
14. Place each quinoa patty in a burger bun along with arugula leaves.
15. Serve with yogurt dill sauce.

Nutrition Info:
- (Per serving) Calories 231 | Fat 9g |Sodium 271mg | Carbs 32.8g | Fiber 6.4g | Sugar 7g | Protein 6.3g

Desserts Recipes

Air Fryer Sweet Twists	64
Grilled Peaches	64
Bread Pudding	65
Brownie Muffins	65
Lemony Sweet Twists	66
Lemon Sugar Cookie Bars Monster Sugar Cookie Bars	66
Chocolate Chip Muffins	67
Cinnamon Bread Twists	67
Fried Dough With Roasted Strawberries	68
Apple Crisp	68
Cinnamon-sugar "churros" With Caramel Sauce	69
Fudge Brownies	69
Air Fried Bananas	70
S'mores Dip With Cinnamon-sugar Tortillas	70

Desserts Recipes

Air Fryer Sweet Twists

Servings:2 | Cooking Time:9

Ingredients:
- 1 box store-bought puff pastry
- ½ teaspoon cinnamon
- ½ teaspoon sugar
- ½ teaspoon black sesame seeds
- Salt, pinch
- 2 tablespoons Parmesan cheese, freshly grated

Directions:
1. Place the dough on a work surface.
2. Take a small bowl and mix cheese, sugar, salt, sesame seeds, and cinnamon.
3. Press this mixture on both sides of the dough.
4. Now, cut the pastry into 1" x 3" strips.
5. Twist each of the strips 2 times and then lay it onto the flat.
6. Transfer to both the air fryer baskets.
7. Select zone 1 to air fry mode at 400 degrees F for 9-10 minutes.
8. Select the MATCH button for the zone 2 basket.
9. Once cooked, serve.

Nutrition Info:
- (Per serving) Calories 140| Fat9.4g| Sodium 142mg | Carbs 12.3g | Fiber0.8 g | Sugar 1.2g | Protein 2g

Grilled Peaches

Servings: 2 | Cooking Time: 5 Minutes

Ingredients:
- 2 yellow peaches, peeled and cut into wedges
- ¼ cup graham cracker crumbs
- ¼ cup brown sugar
- ¼ cup butter diced into tiny cubes
- Whipped cream or ice cream

Directions:
1. Toss peaches with crumbs, brown sugar, and butter in a bowl.
2. Spread the peaches in one air fryer basket.
3. Return the air fryer basket to the Ninja Foodi 2 Baskets Air Fryer.
4. Choose the "Air Fry" mode for Zone 1 and set the temperature to 350 degrees F and 5 minutes of cooking time.
5. Initiate cooking by pressing the START/PAUSE BUTTON.
6. Serve the peaches with a scoop of ice cream.

Nutrition Info:
- (Per serving) Calories 327 | Fat 14.2g |Sodium 672mg | Carbs 47.2g | Fiber 1.7g | Sugar 24.8g | Protein 4.4g

Bread Pudding

Servings: 4 | Cooking Time: 15 Minutes

Ingredients:
- 2 cups bread cubes
- 1 egg
- ⅔ cup heavy cream
- ½ teaspoon vanilla extract
- ¼ cup sugar
- ¼ cup chocolate chips

Directions:
1. Grease two 4 inches baking dish with a cooking spray.
2. Divide the bread cubes in the baking dishes and sprinkle chocolate chips on top.
3. Beat egg with cream, sugar and vanilla in a bowl.
4. Divide this mixture in the baking dishes.
5. Place one pan in each air fryer basket.
6. Return the air fryer basket 1 to Zone 1, and basket 2 to Zone 2 of the Ninja Foodi 2-Basket Air Fryer.
7. Choose the "Air Fry" mode for Zone 1 at 350 degrees F and 15 minutes of cooking time.
8. Select the "MATCH COOK" option to copy the settings for Zone 2.
9. Initiate cooking by pressing the START/PAUSE BUTTON.
10. Allow the pudding to cool and serve.

Nutrition Info:
- (Per serving) Calories 149 | Fat 1.2g | Sodium 3mg | Carbs 37.6g | Fiber 5.8g | Sugar 29g | Protein 1.1g

Brownie Muffins

Servings: 10 | Cooking Time: 15 Minutes

Ingredients:
- 2 eggs
- 96g all-purpose flour
- 1 tsp vanilla
- 130g powdered sugar
- 25g cocoa powder
- 37g pecans, chopped
- 1 tsp cinnamon
- 113g butter, melted

Directions:
1. In a bowl, whisk eggs, vanilla, butter, sugar, and cinnamon until well mixed.
2. Add cocoa powder and flour and stir until well combined.
3. Add pecans and fold well.
4. Pour batter into the silicone muffin moulds.
5. Insert a crisper plate in Ninja Foodi air fryer baskets.
6. Place muffin moulds in both baskets.
7. Select zone 1, then select "bake" mode and set the temperature to 360 degrees F for 15 minutes. Press "match" and then "start/stop" to begin.

Nutrition Info:
- (Per serving) Calories 210 | Fat 10.5g | Sodium 78mg | Carbs 28.7g | Fiber 1g | Sugar 20.2g | Protein 2.6g

Lemony Sweet Twists

Servings: 2 | Cooking Time: 9

Ingredients:
- 1 box store-bought puff pastry
- ½ teaspoon lemon zest
- 1 tablespoon of lemon juice
- 2 teaspoons brown sugar
- Salt, pinch
- 2 tablespoons Parmesan cheese, freshly grated

Directions:
1. Put the puff pastry dough on a clean work area.
2. In a bowl, combine Parmesan cheese, brown sugar, salt, lemon zest, and lemon juice.
3. Press this mixture on both sides of the dough.
4. Now, cut the pastry into 1" x 4" strips.
5. Twist each of the strips.
6. Transfer to both the air fryer baskets.
7. Select zone 1 to air fry mode at 400 degrees F for 9-10 minutes.
8. Select match for zone 2 basket.
9. Once cooked, serve and enjoy.

Nutrition Info:
- (Per serving) Calories 156| Fat10g| Sodium 215mg | Carbs 14g | Fiber 0.4g | Sugar3.3 g | Protein 2.8g

Lemon Sugar Cookie Bars Monster Sugar Cookie Bars

Servings: 12 | Cooking Time: 18 Minutes

Ingredients:
- FOR THE LEMON COOKIE BARS
- Grated zest and juice of 1 lemon
- ½ cup granulated sugar
- 4 tablespoons (½ stick) unsalted butter, at room temperature
- 1 large egg yolk
- 1 teaspoon vanilla extract
- ⅛ teaspoon baking powder
- ½ cup plus 2 tablespoons all-purpose flour
- FOR THE MONSTER COOKIE BARS
- ½ cup granulated sugar
- 4 tablespoons (½ stick) unsalted butter, at room temperature
- 1 large egg yolk
- 1 teaspoon vanilla extract
- ⅛ teaspoon baking powder
- ½ cup plus 2 tablespoons all-purpose flour
- ¼ cup rolled oats
- ¼ cup M&M's
- ¼ cup peanut butter chips

Directions:
1. To prep the lemon cookie bars: In a large bowl, rub together the lemon zest and sugar. Add the butter and use a hand mixer to beat until light and fluffy.
2. Beat in the egg yolk, vanilla, and lemon juice. Mix in the baking powder and flour.
3. To prep the monster cookie bars: In a large bowl, with a hand mixer, beat the sugar and butter until light and fluffy.
4. Beat in the egg yolk and vanilla. Mix in the baking powder and flour. Stir in the oats, M&M's, and peanut butter chips.
5. To cook the cookie bars: Line both baskets with aluminum foil. Press the lemon cookie dough into the Zone 1 basket and insert the basket in the unit. Press the monster cookie dough into the Zone 2 basket and insert the basket in the unit.
6. Select Zone 1, select BAKE, set the temperature to 330°F, and set the timer to 18 minutes. Press MATCH COOK to match Zone 2 settings to Zone 1.
7. Press START/PAUSE to begin cooking.
8. When cooking is complete, the cookies should be set in the middle and have begun to pull away from the sides of the basket.
9. Let the cookies cool completely, about 1 hour. Cut each basket into 6 bars for a total of 12 bars.

Nutrition Info:
- (Per serving) Calories: 191; Total fat: 8.5g; Saturated fat: 5g; Carbohydrates: 27g; Fiber: 0.5g; Protein: 2g; Sodium: 3mg

Chocolate Chip Muffins

Servings: 2 | Cooking Time: 15

Ingredients:
- Salt, pinch
- 2 eggs
- 1/3 cup brown sugar
- 1/3 cup butter
- 4 tablespoons of milk
- ¼ teaspoon of vanilla extract
- ½ teaspoon of baking powder
- 1 cup all-purpose flour
- 1 pouch chocolate chips, 35 grams

Directions:
1. Take 4 oven-safe ramekins that are the size of a cup and layer them with muffin papers.
2. In a bowl, whisk the egg, brown sugar, butter, milk, and vanilla extract.
3. Whisk it all very well with an electric hand beater.
4. Now, in a second bowl, mix the flour, baking powder, and salt.
5. Now, mix the dry ingredients slowly into the wet ingredients.
6. Now, at the end fold in the chocolate chips and mix them well
7. Divide this batter into 4 ramekins.
8. Now, divide it between both zones.
9. Set the time for zone 1 to 15 minutes at 350 degrees F, at AIRFRY mode.
10. Select the MATCH button for the zone 2 basket.
11. Check if not done, and let it AIR FRY for one more minute.
12. Once it is done, serve.

Nutrition Info:
- (Per serving) Calories 757| Fat40.3g| Sodium 426mg | Carbs 85.4g | Fiber 2.2g | Sugar 30.4g | Protein 14.4g

Cinnamon Bread Twists

Servings: 4 | Cooking Time: 15 Minutes

Ingredients:
- Bread Twists Dough
- 120g all-purpose flour
- 1 teaspoon baking powder
- ¼ teaspoon salt
- 150g fat free Greek yogurt
- Brushing
- 2 tablespoons light butter
- 2 tablespoons granulated sugar
- 1-2 teaspoons ground cinnamon, to taste

Directions:
1. Mix flour, salt and baking powder in a bowl.
2. Stir in yogurt and the rest of the dough ingredients in a bowl.
3. Mix well and make 8 inches long strips out of this dough.
4. Twist the strips and place them in the air fryer baskets.
5. Return the air fryer basket 1 to Zone 1, and basket 2 to Zone 2 of the Ninja Foodi 2-Basket Air Fryer.
6. Choose the "Air Fry" mode for Zone 1 at 375 degrees F and 15 minutes of cooking time.
7. Select the "MATCH COOK" option to copy the settings for Zone 2.
8. Initiate cooking by pressing the START/PAUSE BUTTON.
9. Flip the twists once cooked halfway through.
10. Mix butter with cinnamon and sugar in a bowl.
11. Brush this mixture over the twists.
12. Serve.

Nutrition Info:
- (Per serving) Calories 391 | Fat 24g |Sodium 142mg | Carbs 38.5g | Fiber 3.5g | Sugar 21g | Protein 6.6g

Fried Dough With Roasted Strawberries

Servings: 4 | Cooking Time: 20 Minutes

Ingredients:
- FOR THE FRIED DOUGH
- 6 ounces refrigerated pizza dough, at room temperature
- 2 tablespoons all-purpose flour, for dusting
- 4 tablespoons vegetable oil
- 2 tablespoons powdered sugar
- FOR THE ROASTED STRAWBERRIES
- 2 cups frozen whole strawberries
- 2 tablespoons granulated sugar

Directions:
1. To prep the fried dough: Divide the dough into four equal portions.
2. Dust a clean work surface with the flour. Place one dough portion on the surface and use a rolling pin to roll to a ⅛-inch thickness. Rub both sides of the dough with 1 tablespoon of oil. Repeat with remaining dough portions and oil.
3. To prep the strawberries: Place the strawberries in the Zone 2 basket. Sprinkle the granulated sugar on top.
4. To cook the fried dough and strawberries: Install a crisper plate in the Zone 1 basket. Place 2 dough portions in the basket and insert the basket in the unit. Insert the Zone 2 basket in the unit.
5. Select Zone 1, select AIR FRY, set the temperature to 400°F, and set the timer to 18 minutes.
6. Select Zone 2, select ROAST, set the temperature to 330°F, and set the timer to 20 minutes. Select SMART FINISH.
7. Press START/PAUSE to begin cooking.
8. When both timers read 8 minutes, press START/PAUSE. Remove the Zone 1 basket and transfer the fried dough to a cutting board. Place the 2 remaining dough portions in the basket, then reinsert the basket. Remove the Zone 2 basket and stir the strawberries. Reinsert the basket and press START/PAUSE to resume cooking.
9. When cooking is complete, the dough should be cooked through and the strawberries soft and jammy.
10. Sprinkle the fried dough with powdered sugar. Gently mash the strawberries with a fork. Spoon the strawberries onto each fried dough portion and serve.

Nutrition Info:
- (Per serving) Calories: 304; Total fat: 15g; Saturated fat: 2.5g; Carbohydrates: 38g; Fiber: 0.5g; Protein: 3g; Sodium: 421mg

Apple Crisp

Servings: 8 | Cooking Time: 14 Minutes.

Ingredients:
- 3 cups apples, chopped
- 1 tablespoon pure maple syrup
- 2 teaspoons lemon juice
- 3 tablespoons all-purpose flour
- ⅓ cup quick oats
- ¼ cup brown sugar
- 2 tablespoons light butter, melted
- ½ teaspoon cinnamon

Directions:
1. Toss the chopped apples with 1 tablespoon of all-purpose flour, cinnamon, maple syrup, and lemon juice in a suitable bowl.
2. Divide the apples in the two air fryer baskets with their crisper plates.
3. Whisk oats, brown sugar, and remaining all-purpose flour in a small bowl.
4. Stir in melted butter, then divide this mixture over the apples.
5. Return the crisper plate to the Ninja Foodi Dual Zone Air Fryer.
6. Select the Bake mode for Zone 1 and set the temperature to 375 degrees F and the time to 14 minutes.
7. Select the "MATCH" button to copy the settings for Zone 2.
8. Initiate cooking by pressing the START/STOP button.
9. Enjoy fresh.

Nutrition Info:
- (Per serving) Calories 258 | Fat 12.4g | Sodium 79mg | Carbs 34.3g | Fiber 1g | Sugar 17g | Protein 3.2g

Cinnamon-sugar "churros" With Caramel Sauce

Servings:4 | Cooking Time: 10 Minutes

Ingredients:
- FOR THE "CHURROS"
- 1 sheet frozen puff pastry, thawed
- Butter-flavored cooking spray
- 1 tablespoon granulated sugar
- 1 teaspoon ground cinnamon
- FOR THE CARAMEL SAUCE
- ½ cup packed light brown sugar
- 2 tablespoons unsalted butter, cut into small pieces
- ¼ cup heavy (whipping) cream
- 2 teaspoons vanilla extract
- ⅛ teaspoon kosher salt

Directions:
1. To prep the "churros": Cut the puff pastry crosswise into 4 rectangles. Fold each piece in half lengthwise to make a long thin "churro."
2. To prep the caramel sauce: Measure the brown sugar, butter, cream, and vanilla into an ovenproof ramekin or bowl (no need to stir).
3. To cook the "churros" and caramel sauce: Install a crisper plate in the Zone 1 basket. Place the "churros" in the basket and insert the basket in the unit. Place the ramekin in the Zone 2 basket and insert the basket in the unit.
4. Select Zone 1, select AIR FRY, set the temperature to 330°F, and set the timer to 10 minutes.
5. Select Zone 2, select BAKE, set the temperature to 350°F, and set the timer to 10 minutes. Select SMART FINISH.
6. Press START/PAUSE to begin cooking.
7. When the Zone 2 timer reads 5 minutes, press START/PAUSE. Remove the basket and stir the caramel. Reinsert the basket and press START/PAUSE to resume cooking.
8. When cooking is complete, the "churros" will be golden brown and cooked through and the caramel sauce smooth.
9. Spritz each "churro" with cooking spray and sprinkle generously with the granulated sugar and cinnamon.
10. Stir the salt into the caramel sauce. Let cool for 5 to 10 minutes before serving. Note that the caramel will thicken as it cools.

Nutrition Info:
- (Per serving) Calories: 460; Total fat: 26g; Saturated fat: 14g; Carbohydrates: 60g; Fiber: 1.5g; Protein: 5g; Sodium: 254mg

Fudge Brownies

Servings:4 | Cooking Time:16

Ingredients:
- 1/2 cup all-purpose flour
- 1/4 cup unsweetened cocoa powder
- 3/4 teaspoon kosher salt
- 2 large eggs, whisked
- 1 tablespoon almond milk
- 1/2 cup brown sugar
- 1/2 cup packed white sugar
- 1/2 tablespoon vanilla extract
- 8 ounces of semisweet chocolate chips, melted
- 2/4 cup unsalted butter, melted

Directions:
1. Take a medium bowl, and use a hand beater to whisk together eggs, milk, both the sugars and vanilla.
2. In a separate microwave-safe bowl, mix melted butter and chocolate and microwave it for 30 seconds to melt the chocolate.
3. Add all the listed dry ingredients to the chocolate mixture.
4. Now incorporate the egg bowl ingredient into the batter.
5. Spray a reasonable size round baking pan that fits in baskets of air fryer
6. Grease the pan with cooking spray.
7. Now pour the batter into the pan, put the crisper plate in baskets.
8. Add the pans and insert the basket into the unit.
9. Select the AIR FRY mode and adjust the setting the temperature to 300 degrees F, for 30 minutes.
10. Check it after 35 minutes and if not done, cook for 10 more minutes
11. Once it's done, take it out and let it get cool before serving.
12. Enjoy.

Nutrition Info:
- (Per serving) Calories 760| Fat43.3 g| Sodium644 mg | Carbs 93.2g | Fiber5.3 g | Sugar 70.2g | Protein 6.2g

Air Fried Bananas

Servings: 4 | Cooking Time: 13 Minutes.

Ingredients:
- 4 bananas, sliced
- 1 avocado oil cooking spray

Directions:
1. Spread the banana slices in the two crisper plates in a single layer.
2. Drizzle avocado oil over the banana slices.
3. Return the crisper plate to the Ninja Foodi Dual Zone Air Fryer.
4. Choose the Air Fry mode for Zone 1 and set the temperature to 350 degrees F and the time to 13 minutes.
5. Select the "MATCH" button to copy the settings for Zone 2.
6. Initiate cooking by pressing the START/STOP button.
7. Serve.

Nutrition Info:
- (Per serving) Calories 149 | Fat 1.2g |Sodium 3mg | Carbs 37.6g | Fiber 5.8g | Sugar 29g | Protein 1.1g

S'mores Dip With Cinnamon-sugar Tortillas

Servings:4 | Cooking Time: 5 Minutes

Ingredients:
- FOR THE S'MORES DIP
- ½ cup chocolate-hazelnut spread
- ¼ cup milk chocolate or white chocolate chips
- ¼ cup graham cracker crumbs
- ½ cup mini marshmallows
- FOR THE CINNAMON-SUGAR TORTILLAS
- 4 (6-inch) flour tortillas
- Butter-flavored cooking spray
- 1 teaspoon granulated sugar
- ½ teaspoon ground cinnamon
- ¼ teaspoon ground cardamom (optional)

Directions:
1. To prep the s'mores dip: Spread the chocolate- hazelnut spread in the bottom of a shallow ovenproof ramekin or dish.
2. Scatter the chocolate chips and graham cracker crumbs over the top. Arrange the marshmallows in a single layer on top of the crumbs.
3. To prep the tortillas: Spray both sides of each tortilla with cooking spray. Cut each tortilla into 8 wedges and sprinkle both sides evenly with sugar, cinnamon, and cardamom (if using).
4. To cook the dip and tortillas: Install a crisper plate in each of the two baskets. Place the ramekin in the Zone 1 basket and insert the basket in the unit. Place the tortillas in the Zone 2 basket and insert the basket in the unit.
5. Select Zone 1, select BAKE, set the temperature to 330°F, and set the timer to 5 minutes.
6. Select Zone 2, select AIR FRY, set the temperature to 375°F, and set the timer to 5 minutes. Select SMART FINISH.
7. Press START/PAUSE to begin cooking.
8. When the Zone 2 timer reads 3 minutes, press START/PAUSE. Remove the basket and shake it to redistribute the chips. Reinsert the basket and press START/PAUSE to resume cooking.
9. When cooking is complete, the dip will be bubbling and golden brown and the chips crispy.
10. If desired, toast the marshmallows more: Select Zone 1, select AIR BROIL, set the temperature to 450°F, and set the timer to 1 minute. Cook until the marshmallows are deep golden brown.
11. Let the dip cool for 2 to 3 minutes. Serve with the cinnamon-sugar tortilla chips.

Nutrition Info:
- (Per serving) Calories: 404; Total fat: 18g; Saturated fat: 7g; Carbohydrates: 54g; Fiber: 2.5g; Protein: 6g; Sodium: 346mg

Recipe ....

From the kicthen of ....

Serves .... Prep time .... Cook time ....

☐ Difficulty   ☐ Easy   ☐ Medium   ☐ Hard

Ingredient

....
....
....
....
....

Directions ....

....
....
....
....
....

APPENDIX A: Measurement Conversions

BASIC KITCHEN CONVERSIONS & EQUIVALENTS

DRY MEASUREMENTS CONVERSION CHART

3 TEASPOONS = 1 TABLESPOON = 1/16 CUP

6 TEASPOONS = 2 TABLESPOONS = 1/8 CUP

12 TEASPOONS = 4 TABLESPOONS = 1/4 CUP

24 TEASPOONS = 8 TABLESPOONS = 1/2 CUP

36 TEASPOONS = 12 TABLESPOONS = 3/4 CUP

48 TEASPOONS = 16 TABLESPOONS = 1 CUP

METRIC TO US COOKING CONVERSIONS

OVEN TEMPERATURES

120 °C = 250 °F

160 °C = 320 °F

180° C = 350 °F

205 °C = 400 °F

220 °C = 425 °F

LIQUID MEASUREMENTS CONVERSION CHART

8 FLUID OUNCES = 1 CUP = 1/2 PINT = 1/4 QUART

16 FLUID OUNCES = 2 CUPS = 1 PINT = 1/2 QUART

32 FLUID OUNCES = 4 CUPS = 2 PINTS = 1 QUART

 = 1/4 GALLON

128 FLUID OUNCES = 16 CUPS = 8 PINTS = 4 QUARTS = 1 GALLON

BAKING IN GRAMS

1 CUP FLOUR = 140 GRAMS

1 CUP SUGAR = 150 GRAMS

1 CUP POWDERED SUGAR = 160 GRAMS

1 CUP HEAVY CREAM = 235 GRAMS

VOLUME

1 MILLILITER = 1/5 TEASPOON

5 ML = 1 TEASPOON

15 ML = 1 TABLESPOON

240 ML = 1 CUP OR 8 FLUID OUNCES

1 LITER = 34 FL. OUNCES

WEIGHT

1 GRAM = .035 OUNCES

100 GRAMS = 3.5 OUNCES

500 GRAMS = 1.1 POUNDS

1 KILOGRAM = 35 OUNCES

US TO METRIC COOKING CONVERSIONS

1/5 TSP = 1 ML

1 TSP = 5 ML

1 TBSP = 15 ML

1 FL OUNCE = 30 ML

1 CUP = 237 ML

1 PINT (2 CUPS) = 473 ML

1 QUART (4 CUPS) = .95 LITER

1 GALLON (16 CUPS) = 3.8 LITERS

1 OZ = 28 GRAMS

1 POUND = 454 GRAMS

BUTTER

1 CUP BUTTER = 2 STICKS = 8 OUNCES = 230 GRAMS = 8 TABLESPOONS

WHAT DOES 1 CUP EQUAL

1 CUP = 8 FLUID OUNCES

1 CUP = 16 TABLESPOONS

1 CUP = 48 TEASPOONS

1 CUP = 1/2 PINT

1 CUP = 1/4 QUART

1 CUP = 1/16 GALLON

1 CUP = 240 ML

BAKING PAN CONVERSIONS

1 CUP ALL-PURPOSE FLOUR = 4.5 OZ

1 CUP ROLLED OATS = 3 OZ 1 LARGE EGG = 1.7 OZ

1 CUP BUTTER = 8 OZ 1 CUP MILK = 8 OZ

1 CUP HEAVY CREAM = 8.4 OZ

1 CUP GRANULATED SUGAR = 7.1 OZ

1 CUP PACKED BROWN SUGAR = 7.75 OZ

1 CUP VEGETABLE OIL = 7.7 OZ

1 CUP UNSIFTED POWDERED SUGAR = 4.4 OZ

BAKING PAN CONVERSIONS

9-INCH ROUND CAKE PAN = 12 CUPS

10-INCH TUBE PAN =16 CUPS

11-INCH BUNDT PAN = 12 CUPS

9-INCH SPRINGFORM PAN = 10 CUPS

9 X 5 INCH LOAF PAN = 8 CUPS

9-INCH SQUARE PAN = 8 CUPS

Appendix B : Recipes Index

A

Air Fried Bananas   70
Air Fryer Sweet Twists   64
Almond Chicken   39
Apple Crisp   68
Avocado Fries With Sriracha Dip   22

B

Bacon Potato Patties   58
Bacon Wrapped Corn Cob   57
Bacon Wrapped Stuffed Chicken   37
Bacon-wrapped Dates Bacon-wrapped Scallops   21
Bacon-wrapped Shrimp   52
Baked Mushroom And Mozzarella Frittata With Breakfast Potatoes   17
Balsamic Duck Breast   43
Banana And Raisins Muffins   11
Beef & Broccoli   29
Beef Jerky Pineapple Jerky   25
Beef Kofta Kebab   33
Bread Pudding   65
Breakfast Bacon   10
Breakfast Frittata   13
Broiled Teriyaki Salmon With Eggplant In Stir-fry Sauce   49
Brownie Muffins   65
Brussels Sprouts   62

C

Cauliflower Cheese Patties   19
Cauliflower Gnocchi   20
Cheese Stuffed Mushrooms   26
Chicken Parmesan   40
Chicken Potatoes   43
Chicken Tenders And Curly Fries   42
Chickpea Fritters   61
Chinese Bbq Pork   35
Chocolate Chip Muffins   67
Cinnamon Bread Twists   67
Cinnamon Sugar Chickpeas   22
Cinnamon-raisin Bagels Everything Bagels   14
Cinnamon-sugar "churros" With Caramel Sauce   69
Crab Rangoon Dip With Crispy Wonton Strips   24

Crispy Catfish   48
Crispy Hash Browns   12
Crispy Popcorn Shrimp   26
Crispy Sesame Chicken   40
Curry-crusted Lamb Chops With Baked Brown Sugar Acorn Squash   30

D

Delicious Haddock   47
Donuts   11

E

Egg White Muffins   16

F

Fish Sandwich   50
Fresh Mix Veggies In Air Fryer   61
Fried Avocado Tacos   60
Fried Dough With Roasted Strawberries   68
Fried Olives   55
Fried Ravioli   24
Fried Tilapia   50
Fudge Brownies   69
Furikake Salmon   49

G

Glazed Scallops   53
Glazed Steak Recipe   31
Green Salad With Crispy Fried Goat Cheese And Baked Croutons   59
Green Tomato Stacks   58
Grilled Peaches   64

H

Hash Browns   10
Healthy Oatmeal Muffins   15

I

Italian Sausages With Peppers, Potatoes, And Onions   30
Italian-style Meatballs With Garlicky Roasted Broccoli   32

J

Juicy Duck Breast   37

K

Kale And Spinach Chips   55

L

Lamb Chops With Dijon Garlic   34
Lemon Chicken Thighs   38
Lemon Herb Cauliflower   60
Lemon Sugar Cookie Bars Monster Sugar Cookie Bars   66
Lemony Sweet Twists   66
Lime Glazed Tofu   56

M

Marinated Pork Chops   34
Marinated Steak & Mushrooms   35
Meatballs   29
Morning Egg Rolls   15
Mushroom Roll-ups   56
Mustard Rubbed Lamb Chops   33

O

Onion Rings   20
Orange Chicken With Roasted Snap Peas And Scallions   41

P

Peppered Asparagus   19
Perfect Cinnamon Toast   13
Pork With Green Beans And Potatoes   31
Potato Tater Tots   21
Pretzel Chicken Cordon Bleu   39

Q

Quinoa Patties   62

R

Roasted Salmon And Parmesan Asparagus   48

S

S'mores Dip With Cinnamon-sugar Tortillas   70
Salmon Nuggets   52
Sausage With Eggs   12
Seafood Shrimp Omelet   46
Sesame Ginger Chicken   38
Short Ribs & Root Vegetables   32
Shrimp Po'boys With Sweet Potato Fries   53
Smoked Salmon   47
Spicy Chicken Wings   44
Spicy Lamb Chops   28
Spinach Egg Muffins   16
Steak In Air Fry   28
Stuffed Mushrooms   23
Stuffed Tomatoes   59
Sweet And Spicy Carrots With Chicken Thighs   42
Sweet Bites   25
Sweet Potato Hash   14
Sweet Potatoes Hash   17

T

Tasty Parmesan Shrimp   46
Thai Curry Chicken Kabobs   44
Tilapia With Mojo And Crispy Plantains   51
Tofu Veggie Meatballs   23

Z

Zucchini Cakes   57

Printed in Great Britain
by Amazon